ILLUSTRATORS
41

THE SOCIETY OF ILLUSTRATORS 41ST ANNUAL OF AMERICAN ILLUSTRATION

From the exhibition held in the galleries of the
Society of Illustrators Museum of American Illustration
128 East 63rd Street, New York City
February 13 - April 17, 1999

Society of Illustrators, Inc.

128 East 63rd Street, New York, NY 10021-7303

www.societyillustrator.org

ISBN 2-88046-466-8

Library of Congress Catalog Card Number 59-10849

A RotoVision Book

Published and distributed by RotoVision SA

Rue du Bugnon 7

CH-1299 Crans-Près-Céligny

Switzerland

Tel: +41 (22) 776 0511

Fax: +41 (22) 776 0889

RotoVision SA, Sales & Production Office

Sheridan House, 112/116A Western Road

Hove, East Sussex BN3 1DD, UK

Tel. + 44 (0) 1273 72 72 68

Fax + 44 (0) 1273 72 72 69

Distributed to the trade in the United States by:

Butterworth Hienemann

225 Wildwood Avenue

Woburn, MA 01801-2041

Tel: +1 (781) 904-2632

Fax: +1 (781) 904-2630

Jill Bossert, Editor

Bernadette Evangelist, Designer

Cover painting by John Rush

Production and separations in Singapore by ProVision Pte. Ltd.

Tel: +65 334 7720

Fax: +65 334 7721

Photo Credits: Joe Ciardiello by ©Tony Troiano (Orazio Fotografik),

Lucinda Levine by Jake Levine, Ted Lewin by Betsy Lewin, Stanley Meltzoff by Henry Grosskinsky,

Joseph Montebello by Helen Marcus, Francoise Mouly by © Gaspar Tringale,

Barbara Nessim by Heather McGuire ©, Rafal Olbinski by Susumu Sato ©,

Simms Taback by Robert Storm

CHAIRMAN'S MESSAGE

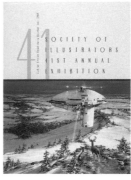

My first encounter with the Society's Annual Exhibition was some thirty-six years ago. Then a young art student, I was simultaneously inspired and intimidated. It seemed an utter impossibility to imagine that one day my work would hang among the distinguished few whose work represents the best examples of the illustrators' craft. Somewhere in that long journey through the years, I'd forgotten the thrill these shows would induce—and I must confess, there were times when I wasn't an enthusiastic supporter of these efforts. The experience of chairing this show has been both a great honor and a keen reminder of how marvelously talented a breed illustrators are, and how vitally important their work is in the sometimes uneasy union of art and commerce.

This, then, is what carefully selected and balanced juries of talented and dedicated art professionals have selected as the benchmark of quality for the field. With the millennium fast approaching it is clear that change is in the wind. How the illustration markets will be affected by that change might well be mirrored in these pages, for those wise enough to discern the signs.

In an endeavor of this magnitude there are many people to thank. I am indebted to my Assistant Chair Martha Vaughan and Past Chair Murray Tinkelman for their inexhaustible patience, tireless efforts and judicious counsel. I am truly fortunate to count them among my dearest friends. The immense talents of artist John Berkey and designer Wendell Minor combined to create one of the most unique Call for Entries posters in Society history, and one befitting the new millennium. Thanks too, to the jurors and the Society staff for their dedication to making *Illustrators 41* truly the best of its kind. And, finally, thank you to the many artists who submitted their work, whose art appears in these pages, and who have faithfully supported this exhibition. They are an inspiration to us all.

Vincent Di Fate
Chairman,
41st Annual Exhibition

Portrait by Roger Kastel

THE SOCIETY OF ILLUSTRATORS 41ST ANNUAL OF AMERICAN ILLUSTRATION AWARDS PRESENTATIONS

Chairman Vincent Di Fate with American Showcase representatives Joe Safferson and John Bergstrom. American Showcase was once again the Exclusive Sponsor of the Annual Exhibition Awards Galas.

american **showcase**

THE ILLUSTRATORS HALL OF FAME

Since 1958, the Society of Illustrators has elected to its Hall of Fame artists recognized for their "distinguished achievement in the art of illustration." The list of previous winners is truly a "Who's Who" of illlustation. Former Presidents of the Society meet annually to elect those who will be so honored.

HALL OF FAME COMMITTEE 1999

Murray Tinkelman, *Chairman*

Willis Pyle, *Chairman Emeritus*

Former Presidents
Vincent Di Fate
Diane Dillon
Peter Fiore
Charles McVicker
Wendell Minor
Howard Munce
Alvin J. Pimsler
Warren Rogers
Eileen Hedy Schultz
Shannon Stirnweis
David K. Stone
John Witt

HALL OF FAME LAUREATES 1999

Mitchell Hooks
Stanley Meltzoff
Andrew Loomis*
Antonio Lopez*
Thomas Moran*
Rose O'Neill*
Adolph Treidler*

HALL OF FAME LAUREATES 1958-1997

1958	Norman Rockwell
1959	Dean Cornwell
1959	Harold Von Schmidt
1960	Fred Cooper
1961	Floyd Davis
1962	Edward Wilson
1963	Walter Biggs
1964	Arthur William Brown

1965	Al Parker
1966	Al Dorne
1967	Robert Fawcett
1968	Peter Helck
1969	Austin Briggs
1970	Rube Goldberg
1971	Stevan Dohanos
1972	Ray Prohaska
1973	Jon Whitcomb
1974	Tom Lovell
1974	Charles Dana Gibson*
1974	N.C. Wyeth*
1975	Bernie Fuchs
1975	Maxfield Parrish*
1975	Howard Pyle*
1976	John Falter
1976	Winslow Homer*
1976	Harvey Dunn*
1977	Robert Peak
1977	Wallace Morgan*
1977	J.C. Leyendecker*
1978	Coby Whitmore
1978	Norman Price*
1978	Frederic Remington*
1979	Ben Stahl
1979	Edwin Austin Abbey*
1979	Lorraine Fox*
1980	Saul Tepper
1980	Howard Chandler Christy*
1980	James Montgomery Flagg*
1981	Stan Galli
1981	Frederic R. Gruger*
1981	John Gannam*
1982	John Clymer
1982	Henry P. Raleigh*
1982	Eric (Carl Erickson)*
1983	Mark English
1983	Noel Sickles*
1983	Franklin Booth*
1984	Neysa Moran McMein*
1984	John LaGatta*
1984	James Williamson*
1985	Charles Marion Russell*
1985	Arthur Burdett Frost*
1985	Robert Weaver
1986	Rockwell Kent*

1986	Al Hirschfeld
1987	Haddon Sundblom*
1987	Maurice Sendak
1988	René Bouché*
1988	Pruett Carter*
1988	Robert T. McCall
1989	Erté
1989	John Held Jr.*
1989	Arthur Ignatius Keller*
1990	Burt Silverman
1990	Robert Riggs*
1990	Morton Roberts*
1991	Donald Teague
1991	Jessie Willcox Smith*
1991	William A. Smith*
1992	Joe Bowler
1992	Edwin A. Georgi*
1992	Dorothy Hood*
1993	Robert McGinnis
1993	Thomas Nast*
1993	Coles Phillips*
1994	Harry Anderson
1994	Elizabeth Shippen Green*
1994	Ben Shahn*
1995	James Avati
1995	McClelland Barclay*
1995	Joseph Clement Coll*
1995	Frank E. Schoonover*
1996	Herb Tauss
1996	Anton Otto Fischer*
1996	Winsor McCay*
1996	Violet Oakley*
1996	Mead Schaeffer*
1997	Diane and Leo Dillon
1997	Frank McCarthy
1997	Chesley Bonestell*
1997	Joe DeMers*
1997	Maynard Dixon*
1997	Harrison Fisher*
1998	Robert M. Cunningham
1998	Frank Frazetta
1998	Boris Artzybasheff *
1998	Kerr Eby*
1998	Edward Penfield*
1998	Martha Sawyers*

*Presented posthumously

HALL OF FAME 1999

ANDREW LOOMIS 1892-1952

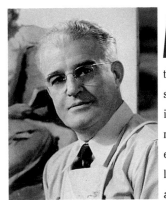

Andrew Loomis readily understood the power of straightforward illustrative communication. An energetic, popular advertising and story illustrator, Loomis also authored a number of the landmark art technique texts. In his *Creative Illustration* he writes: "It can be taken as a sound rule that the simpler the presentation of a subject, the better it will be pictorially. This is the secret of good advertising material or any subjects seeking to command attention."

The period of Loomis's greatest visibility, from the early 1920s through the late 1940s, witnessed an explosion in what we now call "the mass market." It was only with the arrival of the 1920s that the combining of the best illustration with nationally distributed products achieved prominence. Loomis, through his carefully composed paintings and richly romantic imagery, helped speed the movement. In his book *Figure Drawing for All It's Worth*, Loomis summed up his approach by saying, "There is no other course than somehow to go beyond the obvious fact to pertinent fact, to characterization, to the emotional and dramatic, to selection and taste, to simplification, subordination and accentuation. It is 10% how you draw and 90% what you draw."

He approached his story assignments in much the same way, believing "the keynote of the [story] illustrator's job [is] to sell the story, just as he would any product." For Loomis, illustration was a continuing process of growth tied inextricably to society's constant changing. As he wrote in *Creative Illustration*: "Illustration must encompass emotion, the life we live, the things we do and how we feel." In *Successful Drawing* he stressed the need for a personal approach to the creative life: "...one's skill is never complete, one's knowledge is forever lacking, one's taste is invariably altered, one's opinion ever subject to controversy. There is a complete and constant urge toward improvement. Painting is nearer to life than any other form of art."

Throughout his more-than-thirty-year career he remained a dedicated craftsman, a respected teacher and an eager student. Forty years after his death, his impact is felt to this day.

Fred Taraba

Illustration for Coca-Cola advertisement. Courtesy Illustration House.

HALL OF FAME 1999

ANTONIO LOPEZ 1943-1987

Antonio Lopez, born in Puerto Rico in 1943, was transplanted to New York's Spanish Harlem at the age of eight. He was quoted as saying he felt his vocation was determined when a rich Spanish aunt arrived in Puerto Rico in summer wearing a fur coat and alligator shoes. "Alligators into shoes! That's what did it to me—it had something to do with extremes." His conception of feminine beauty was influenced by his mother's exotic arching cheekbones and developed into a pan-cultural, multi-ethnic idea. As a child in El Barrio, he drew his mother in dresses he had made for her.

Antonio graduated from the High School of Art and Design and then attended the Fashion Institute of Technology where he met fellow artist Juan Ramos. They remained partners for 25 years, with Juan serving as Antonio's art director and alter ego. In 1962, Antonio began working full-time for *Women's Wear Daily* as one of their youngest illustrators. Within a year, he left *WWD* to pursue a successful freelance career. His dyanamic style put a whole new kind of sexy, streetwise energy into the field of fashion illustration. His influences were diverse, ranging from Old Masters to Pop Art, Surrealism, Cubism, Constructivism, comic strips, and pinups from the 1940s.

Antonio's editorial illustrations appeared regularly in *The New York Times Sunday Magazine*, as well as the American, Italian, French, and Japanese editions of *Vogue* and numerous other international high fashion magazines. The advertising illustration he did regularly for Bloomingdale's and Bergdorf Goodman was a staple in the daily *New York Times*. Antonio lived and worked in Japan in 1970 which resulted in campaigns for La

Foret Department Stores in the ensuing years. He spent most of the 1970s in Paris where his life at the center of the fashion world was like a continual costume party. He always worked from life, and his models—who were his muses—included Jerry Hall, Pat Cleveland, Jessica Lange, Grace Jones, and Tina Chow.

"More than describing clothes," wrote *GQ* editor Phillip Smith in *Arts* magazine in 1980, "the drawings are about a feeling of being that comes from living and looking a certain way. The images function more as social icons than advertisement."

The year 1982 saw the publication of *Antonio's Girls*, a collection of his illustrations from 1974 to 1982. In 1983 the Council of Fashion Designers of America named Antonio as American Fashion Illustrator of the Year. In 1985 he published *Antonio's Tales from the Thousand and One Nights*. During the last ten years of his life, Antonio devoted much of his time to giving lectures and workshops to students of fashion illustration. He told an interviewer, "I'm always inspired by people. People are what I love more than anything else."

Judy Francis

Illustration for Vanity Fair, *1980s, fourth in a surreal robe series. Gift of Juan Ramos, illustration from the Frances Neady Collection, Fashion Institute of Technology.*

HALL OF FAME 1999

THOMAS MORAN 1837-1926

The name Thomas Moran comes to mind when one thinks of the "Great American Landscape." We think of Moran the painter, not the illustrator.

Yet during his lifetime he produced some two thousand illustrations for such publications as *Scribner's Monthly*, *Harper's Weekly*, and *The Century*. It is true that Moran will forever be remembered as one of the finest landscape painters in America, but his contribution to the art of illustration measures with the best.

Scribner's Monthly published 14 Moran ink-and-wash drawings for a Nathaniel P. Langford article, "Wonders of the Yellowstone," in May of 1871. This singular article, with beautifully engraved adaptations of Moran's drawings, changed the course of the young artist's life and the course of American history. Moran, the Easterner, discovered his destiny in the American West, and the United States Government created Yellowstone as our first national park in March of 1872. Moran, the illustrator, had proven that a printed image on a page provided the ultimate form of communication for America to know its own frontier.

Born February 12th, 1837, in Lancashire, England, young Thomas emigrated to America at the age of seven with his mother Mary, five brothers, and two sisters to join Thomas Moran, Sr. in Philadelphia.

At 16, he apprenticed with a wood engraving firm. This no doubt gave Moran early training in composition and creating pictures with good value structure. He always had his sketchbook in hand, recording the beauty of his surroundings wherever he traveled. His first drawings, which appeared in *Harper's Monthly* in June of 1862, attracted considerable attention. Throughout his life, Moran, the great American landscape painter, continued to contribute to the field of illustration. He never denied the roots of his craft, noting that his fine art was never diminished by creating illustrations for the printed page.

Thomas Moran's legacy is in showing us the spirit found in the natural beauty of the American West. Whether his art was created for a magazine or a gallery wall, he gave his adopted country a gift for the ages, never to be equaled.

Wendell Minor
Hall of Fame Committee

View from Glenora, Stickeen River, Alaska, litho pencil on pebbled surface. Courtesy Illustration House.

HALL OF FAME 1999

ROSE O'NEILL 1874-1944

Without exaggeration, *New Yorker* writer Alexander King described Rose O'Neill's Kewpie as a "dimpled bonanza." The winsome elf had made its creator the highest paid female illustrator of her day with earnings of $1.4 million in 1914 dollars. A self-taught career woman in a male-dominated world, Rose O'Neill was original, eccentric, child-like (though childless), generous to a fault, beautiful, humorous, and strong. She worked from the moment she won a prize from the *Omaha World Journal* at age thirteen.

On her first trip to New York she impressed the magazine editors as well as the fashionable Gray Latham, whom she married in 1896, the year she began a seven-year stint at *Puck*, the all-male humor magazine. Her work also appeared in *Harper's Monthly*, *Illustrated American*, *Harper's Bazaar*, *Twentieth Century Home*, *Good Housekeeping*, and *Frank Leslie's*. For *Cosmopolitan*, O'Neill wrote and illustrated her own fiction. Her many advertising clients included the Rock Island Railroad and Oxydol soap.

She divorced Latham in 1901 and the following year married writer Harry Leon Wilson. Though the marriage lasted only five years, O'Neill illustrated several of Wilson's books and she joined his circle of creative friends who would have an influence on her ideas and her art.

During a European trip in 1905-06, O'Neill found encouragement for her noncommercial work, culminating in an exhibition in Paris in 1906 which led to membership in L'Ecole des Beaux Arts. Her art nouveau, symbolist, mystical style balanced the work that made her internationally world famous and temporarily wealthy.

The Kewpies—little Cupids—made their first appearance in 1909 at the suggestion of Edward Bok, editor of *The Ladies' Home Journal*. For nearly twenty-five years Kewpies appeared there as well as in *Woman's Home Companion*, *Good Housekeeping*, and *Delineator*. In addition, the Kewpies comic strip was syndicated in the 1930s. The doll in all its permutations—at first a bisque confection manufactured in many sizes, then made of celluloid and composition—was universally beloved. There followed innumerable Kewpie spin-offs: tableware, wallpaper, teacups, soap, fabrics, wall plaques, inkwells, vases, ice cream trays and molds, greeting cards, cutouts, door knockers, picture frames, rings, clocks, sterling silver salt and pepper shakers, transfers, stationery, and a number of books

By the end of her life Rose O'Neill had lost her fortune through lavish living and extreme generosity. Her museum in Branford, Missouri, and the faithful thousands who collect Kewpies, keep her name alive.

Jill Bossert
Editor, Illustrators 41

Magazine illustration of Kewpies with the Statue of Liberty. Courtesy Illustration House.

HALL OF FAME 1999

ADOLPH TREIDLER 1886-1981

Photo by Dean Daniel, New York City

The son of a peripatetic gold prospector (who never found it), Adolph Treidler was born in West Cliff, Colorado, but had little formal education since his father was always on the search for the next Eldorado. When the family eventually moved to San Francisco, Adolph was a teenager and had already decided he wanted to be an artist. After a short period of study at the California School of Design he began a long, slow, on-the-job learning process of becoming an illustrator. He first started as a paste-up boy in an ad agency run by Fred Cooper, gravitating next to two years with the *Chicago Sunday Tribune* and thence to New York. There he launched his production career during the halcyon years of poster art which he made the central focus of his work. In that specialty he held his own in the fast company of Edward Penfield, Will Bradley, and C.B. Falls, and won several prizes in poster contests.

During World War I, Treidler was a member of the Division of Pictorial Publicity under the Federal Committee of Public Information, contributing many Liberty Loan and recruiting posters for the war effort. And, during World War II, he became the Chairman of the Society of Illustrators' similar organization under the Pictorial Publicity Committee.

Treidler's other preoccupation was travel, which appropriately complemented his production of posters for clients such as the Furness Steamship Lines, The French Lines, and a long association with the Bermuda government Tourism Office. His other advertising clients were among the most prestigious of his day, including the Pierce-Arrow Automobile Company, The Estay Organ Company, The Victor Talking Machine Company, The Regal Shoe Company, and the Aeolian Company. Treidler also painted covers for national magazines such as *Harper's*, *The Century*, *Collier's*, *Woman's Home Companion*, and *Scribner's*.

Treidler was a stalwart of the Society of Illustrators, eventually becoming a Life Member. He was also a charter member of the Artists Guild, a member of the Art Directors Club, and the Joint Ethics Committee.

Walt Reed
Illustration House

FURNESS LIV-ABOARD BERMUDA CRUISES

Poster illustration. Courtesy Society of Illustrators Museum of American Illustration.

HALL OF FAME 1999

MITCHELL HOOKS (b. 1923)

When I called Mitchell Hooks several months ago to tell him that I was submitting his name to the Hall of Fame Committee for consideration, I cautioned him that there were two factors working against the likelihood of success: one, he was still alive (and considering the alternative, it would be some consolation, should the effort fail); and two, due to the enormous versatility he had demonstrated throughout his career, the committee might not have a clear vision about his work. And therein lies the real secret of Mitchell's remarkable success and longevity as an illustrator.

I know of no one who has more completely transformed and reinvented himself as often and as thoroughly as Mitchell Hooks. He's like Fearless Fosdick—that redoubtable Al Capp parody of Dick Tracy—who could be pelted with bullets until he looked like a Swiss cheese, but who just couldn't be stopped. Think of Mitchell, in a more up-to-date analogy, as something like The Terminator, but with a paintbrush and a somewhat trimmer build. With his impeccable sense of taste and exceptional artistic talent, you have a fair approximation of this remarkably gifted gentleman and the reason why his popularity endures.

Born in Detroit in 1923, Mitchell went to the Cass Technical High School and credits such illustration luminaries as Al Parker, Austin Briggs, and Robert Fawcett as early heroes who attracted his interest toward commercial art. He moved to New York at the end of World War II after his hitch in the Army and took a position at the T.J. Peters studio to learn the craft of illustration. After a period of taking on relatively small, inconsequential assignments, he connected with what would become his key market around 1950, when he did his first paperback cover paintings. His earliest works resembled those of many of his peers until illustration underwent a burst of creative expansion in the late 1950s and early '60s. Mitchell found the art of Bob Peak to be especially remarkable in its bold suggestion of new directions. Peak, Robert Weaver and others were moving illustration away from academically realistic pictures to images with a more impressionistic flavor. Mitchell also credits legendary paperback art director Len Leone, and the former publisher of Bantam Books, Oscar Dystel, for having provided the environment that made it possible for him to do some of his more creative and artistically satisfying work.

In each stage of his stylistic growth, Mitchell quickly found his own voice, his own distinctive touch, that set his work apart and put him among those at the vanguard of the ever-evolving illustration market. Underlying his art throughout its many changes, there has always been a judicious sense of taste and conspicuous and superlative draftsmanship. Of his several styles, I'm personally most fond of his work from the 1960s. In those halcyon days when illustrators would dare to push the envelope on traditional picture making, he was using highly saturated colors in shadows, in combination with an exquisite, impressionistic line and brush technique. By the late 1970s and early '80s, as illustration moved beyond its flirtation with Margritte-like conceptualism, Mitch, who had steadfastly resisted the trend, became something of a photorealist, creating images that were so lifelike in their veracity that they seemed to be more real than any photograph could possibly be. Here, too, was another instance in which he became quickly recognized as a top talent among those painting in the photorealistic style at the time.

And now, as we plunge headlong into the digital revolution, rather than face the changing technology landscape with apprehension and despair, Mitchell has taken the initiative to confront and master the relatively new medium of computer art. In what seemed to me to be a truly surreal telephone conversation some months ago, Mitchell boldly proclaimed, "I love this new medium and I hope never again to have to pick up a paintbrush." While, if true, that statement would amount to an incalculable loss to those of us who love illustration, it is again revealing of the openness to change that is native to Mitchell's temperament which has allowed this vastly talented artist to remain a survivor. Unlike many of the field's current crop of digital artists, Mitchell has not allowed the new medium to transform him. He still produces the kind of distinctive images that are clearly his own and he remains (as is no surprise to those of us who know and have long admired his work) one of the best artists at illustration's cutting edge.

Vincent Di Fate
Chairman,
41st Annual Exhibition

The Thackery Jewels *for Harlequin Books. Courtsey Mitchell Hooks.*

HALL OF FAME 1999

STANLEY MELTZOFF (b. 1917)

Who is more capable of writing about the art of Stanley Meltzoff than someone long familiar with his schooling, his training in art, his writings, his works? Who might be more familiar with his aims than someone who has watched his curiosities and interests grow into pictures. Who could follow his thoughts about the current state of the arts or his own ambitions? Who, after all, is better suited to describe how this picture maker solved the problems set by clients within the circumstances and technologies of his time better than me?

How do I account for the unprecedented variety of my subjects? Steel workers perched on the end of a beam for *Fortune*; Spanish Colonial history for *National Geographic*; the aerodynamics of bird flight as a *Scientific American* cover, an anthology of scenes from ancient Athens; American Civil War battles or society in the Gilded Age for *Life*; a colony of astronauts on the moon for paperback science fiction; a parody of a well-known Norman Rockwell as the national bicentennial telephone book cover for AT&T; or the marlin, tuna and tarpon seen underwater for *Sports Illustrated* and *Field & Stream*.

The variety of creatures, narrative modes, character types, assortment of genres, allusions to other styles and older masters is most unusual. To master even one of these fields would once have taken years of academic schooling and a lifetime of experience. Yet in my time, illustrators were asked to depict anything and everything on short deadlines at fixed fees—images which had to remain readable and vivid within the proportions of a printed page. Drawing by hand had already given way to photography; painted pictures competed with machine-made images which moved

and spoke. So, illustrators used photography as well as all other available resources. Finally, all have been absorbed into computer-enhanced print-outs which have digested every other kind of image. Images themselves have become only a part of a graphic package designed for immediate impact rather than for the long slow gaze with which pictures were once examined. Style and subject in images have continuously changed with the styles in pop music or pop clothing, linked to ever more sophisticated tastes of the market. But style is the maker's self, a self who cannot change so fast. The problem has been how to change and yet remain the same.

During my eighty-two years, I found that no sooner had I learned one set of skills than it lost its public and its publications. Ten years or so was the marketable life of each new technology, the skills it required, the styles and subjects which it encouraged, and the media in which it was used for ever newer demographic groups. No sooner had I learned to do full-color emblemata of the new sciences for *Scientific American* covers, than taste shifted to flat graphic design. Having been accepted as a regular for *The Saturday Evening Post*, the magazine folded. When I had become a frequent contributor to *Life*, then the dominant weekly, it also drowned in the flood of TV images. The rapidity of change made my whole career into a succession of promising failures and aborted starts.

What was I to do? New niches for pictures opened, not quite as illustrations but as images with their own self-contained meanings. The standards of picture making that I had learned from history I put to use in popular art, so that my work is marked more by intelligent picture making than by talent as draughtsman or painter. I painted steelworkers balanced on a beam, riveting amidst the clouds, as if they were part of some Baroque Venetian ceiling. I painted the white feathers of wings in flight as iconographic emblems, anatomized to show how birds defy gravity. This difference in aim and reverence accounts for the way my

paintings look.

When, late in life, I could no longer keep my head above water as an illustrator, I considered things from the point of view of the diver I had always been. I began to depict the strange creatures in the light and space under the sea. In the end I turned wholly to these submersive images: striped marlin in the foam gleaming in the remnants of sunlight; a blue marlin sounding as a diver touches it farewell. These images echo Tiepolo, transposed to a lower octave under water. I had found a way into the submerged realms of art bound by the rules of Nature alone.

Stanley Meltzoff

Swordfish & Mako, for National Geographic. *Courtesy Stanley Meltzoff.*

HAMILTON KING AWARD

The Hamilton King Award, created by Mrs. Hamilton King in memory of her husband through a bequest, is presented annually for the best illustration of the year by a member of the Society. The selection is made by former recipients of this award and may be won only once.

HAMILTON KING AWARD 1965-1999

1965	Paul Calle
1966	Bernie Fuchs
1967	Mark English
1968	Robert Peak
1969	Alan E. Cober
1970	Ray Ameijide
1971	Miriam Schottland
1972	Charles Santore
1973	Dave Blossom
1974	Fred Otnes
1975	Carol Anthony
1976	Judith Jampel
1977	Leo & Diane Dillon
1978	Daniel Schwartz
1979	William Teason
1980	Wilson McLean
1981	Gerald McConnell
1982	Robert Heindel
1983	Robert M. Cunningham
1984	Braldt Bralds
1985	Attila Hejja
1986	Doug Johnson
1987	Kinuko Y. Craft
1988	James McMullan
1989	Guy Billout
1990	Edward Sorel
1991	Brad Holland
1992	Gary Kelley
1993	Jerry Pinkney
1994	John Collier
1995	C.F. Payne
1996	Etienne Delessert
1997	Marshall Arisman
1998	Jack Unruh
1999	Gregory Manchess

1999
GREGORY MANCHESS
(b. 1955)

In 1977 I was a young illustrator and one of the creative partners at Hellman Studios when Greg Manchess arrived on our doorstep, portfolio in hand. I suspect he made the four-hour drive south from the Minneapolis College of Art and Design with some reservation. However, I had few reservations when I opened his portfolio. True, it was student work, a little unfocused and highly derivative of an earlier mentor, David Grove. But the kid could draw! Just about anything, including hands, ears, and cartoons. He was also on his way to figuring out paint.

It didn't take me long to hire him, and that marked the beginning of an enduring friendship. He was a welcome addition to our tightly-knit band of illustrators. We worked hard together. We played hard together. We fed off each other's talents and special skills. As studio artists, we often had to be all things to all clients. Greg was good at that and it served him well as a learning experience.

After three years, he struck out on his own. Although we lost touch somewhat, I watched his progress from afar until the 1990s, when we reconnected. It is with more than just professional respect that I delight in sharing this milestone with him. Greg's work has always commanded professional respect, but in the past few years it has blossomed with a more mature, personal voice. To steal a line from Robert Henri in *The Art Spirit*, "He paints like a man going over the top of a hill, singing."

The energy and integrity Greg brings to all his subjects sets him apart. The most obvious entry won the prize for him this year, and yes, it is a masterful rendition of an Arctic adventure. But personally, I was every bit as taken by his other entries under consideration. To find such exquisite drama in a lonely, nocturnal service station, or the almost heroic action in something as mundane as a FedEx loading dock, is a special achievement. And Greg does it painting after painting after painting!

In an age where technology threatens intimacy and Disney's next project is a retelling of *Treasure Island*—in outer space, no less—it's refreshing to recognize a traditional painter like Greg Manchess, who, through it all, remains true to his roots in Sargent, Wyeth, Cornwell, et al.

Gary Kelley

Nanuk: Lord of the Ice, *Dial Books.* (#74)

EDITORIAL

JURY

Al Lorenz, Chairman
Illustrator

N. Ascencios
Illustrator

Kinuko Y. Craft
Illustrator

Amy Guip
Photographer/Illustrator

Dave Herbick
*Principal, David Herbick
Design*

Ted Lewin
Illustrator/Author

Joseph Montebello
*V.P., Creative Director,
Publishing Director, Illustrated
Books, HarperCollins*

Nancy Sabato
*Art Director, Book Group,
Scholastic, Inc.*

Cathleen Toelke
Illustrator

1 GOLD MEDAL

Artist: **Jeffrey Decoster**

Art Director: Andrew Danish

Client: Stanford Today

Medium: Acrylic on board

Size: 24" x 24"

"I always consider it a blessing to get an assignment where I can draw on personal experience to create the image. For this piece I tried to remember specifically what it feels like to have insomnia. I made this illustration at a time when I was becoming more interested in visceral cues—how an image might make you feel, as opposed to conceptual cues—how an image makes you think. As it turned out, I decided to use multiple strategies to express the subject. For once, it helped that I had to stay up all night to make the deadline."

2 GOLD MEDAL

Artist: **Phil Hale**

Art Directors: Tom Staebler/Kerig Pope

Client: Playboy

"A difficult one, painted twice. My father told me, that if you start to strangle a cat, you had better be willing to finish it. *Playboy* has always been the main forum for many of my favorite illustrations, so my fear of Designer Kerig Pope kept me reasonable, at some cost to the picture itself. It moved quickly into the inappropriately moderate, the premeditated. I don't think that is why Kerig hired me. Once he accepted the piece, I recovered and jumped it up a bit—too late. Additionally, in the printing, the most convincing brushwork got sucked into the gutter—as real a vindication of my cowardice and naiveté as anything else."

3 SILVER MEDAL

Artist: **Mark Ryden**

Art Director: Fred Woodward

Client: Rolling Stone

Medium: Oil on wood panel

"I think Christina Ricci has the most amazing face. Her eyes are captivating. When I invent faces out of my imagination they tend to look like her. I have been a fan of hers for a long time, so when *Rolling Stone* asked me to do her portrait I was very enthusiastic. Fortunately, I was given enough time to do the painting in oil, the medium I prefer to use. With oil, I can put much more subtlety into the painting and give it the care and attention I desire."

4 SILVER MEDAL

Artist: **Chris Sheban**

Art Director: Robin Gilmore-Barnes

Client: The Atlantic Monthly

Medium: Watercolor, pencil on paper

Size: 10" x 15"

"This illustration accompanied the story of a young girl growing up in World War II Germany. She once witnessed a great 'silvery' Zeppelin passing overhead. The impression from that day remained with her long afterward. I wanted the image to have a static, almost 'frozen-in-time' quality to suggest this enduring memory."

5

6

5

Artist: **Brad Holland**

Art Director: Steve Powell

Client: Stanford Business

6

Artist: **Raúl Colón**

Art Director: Andrew Kner

Client: Scenario Magazine

Medium: Watercolor, colored pencil on watercolor paper

7

Artist: **Phil Huling**

Art Directors: John Korpics,
Joe Kimberling

Client: Entertainment Weekly

Medium: Pencil, carbon, oil & ink wash
on Strathmore Bristol

8

Artist: **Tim Bower**

Art Director: Sean Barrow

Client: Individual Investor

Medium: Acrylic on paper

Size: 10" x 8"

9

Artist: **Craig Frazier**

Art Director: Lance Hidy

Client: Harvard Business Review

Medium: Cut paper, digital

Size: 16" x 12"

10

Artist: **Nick Dewar**

Art Director: David O'Connor

Client: Success Magazine

Medium: Acrylic on hardboard

Size: 10" x 8"

11

Artist: **Craig Frazier**

Art Director: Patrick Mitchell

Client: Fast Company

Medium: Cut paper, digital

Size: 16" x 12"

7

8

9

10

11

12

Artist: **Anja Kroencke**

Art Director: Ariel Childs

Client: Wallpaper Magazine

Medium: Mixed on paper

Size: 10" x 8"

13

Artist: **Carter Goodrich**

Art Director: Francoise Mouly

Client: The New Yorker

Medium: Colored pencil, watercolor
   on watercolor board

Size: 19" x 14"

14

Artist: **Mark Ryden**

Art Director: Fred Woodward

Client: Rolling Stone

Medium: Oil on board`

15

Artist: **Jon J. Muth**

Art Director: Andrew Kner

Client: Scenario Magazine

Medium: Mixed on paper

Size: 15" x 11"

16

Artist: **Juliette Borda**

Art Director: Judy Garlan

Client: The Atlantic Monthly

Medium: Gouache on paper

Size: 9" x 12"

12

13

14

15

16

17

Artist: **Juliette Borda**

Art Director: Chrystal Falcioni

Client: JUMP

Medium: Gouache on paper

Size: 12" x 9"

18

Artist: **Sarah Wilkins**

Art Director: Emily Crawford

Client: American Recorder

19

Artist: **Phillip Lardy**

Art Directors: John Korpics,
Joe Kimberling

Client: Entertainment Weekly

20

Artist: **Hiroshi Tanabe**

Art Director: Alden Wallace

Client: Details Magazine

Medium: Mixed on paper

Size: 10" x 8"

17

18

19

20

21

Artist: **Tom Herzberg**

Art Director: Jef Capaldi

Client: American Medical News

Medium: Watercolor on paper

Size: 12" x 11"

22

Artist: **Dugald Stermer**

Art Director: Richard Boddy

Client: Discover Magazine

Medium: Pencil, watercolor on Arches

Size: 11" x 14"

23

Artist: **Dugald Stermer**

Art Director: Richard Boddy

Client: Discover Magazine

Medium: Pencil, watercolor on Arches

Size: 20" x 14"

24

Artist: **Mark Ulriksen**

Art Directors: John Korpics,
George McCalman

Client: Entertainment Weekly

Medium: Acrylic on paper

25

Artist: **Stacy Innerst**

Art Director: Chris Dunleavy

Client: Philadelphia Inquirer Magazine

Medium: Acrylic on board

Size: 11" x 9"

26

Artist: **John Springs**

Art Director: Fred Woodward

Client: Rolling Stone

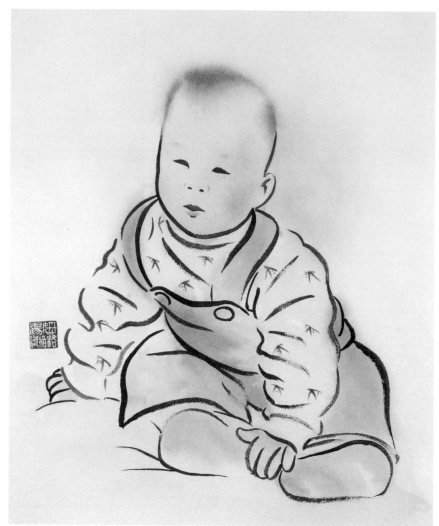

21

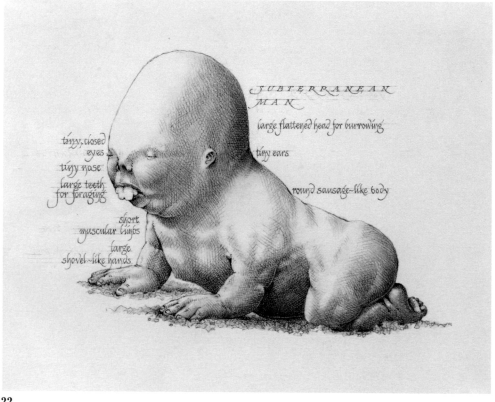

22

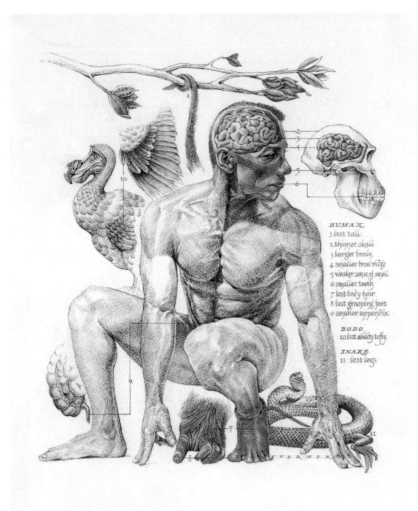

23

24

25

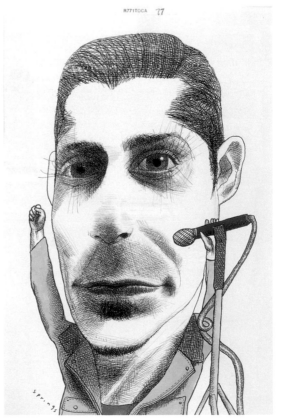

26

27

Artist: **David Hughes**

Art Director: Fred Woodward

Client: Rolling Stone

Medium: Pen & ink, watercolor on paper

28

Artist: **David Hughes**

Art Director: David Matt

Client: Premiere Magazine

Medium: Pen & ink, watercolor on paper

29

Artist: **Philip Burke**

Art Director: Traci Churchill

Client: Your Company Magazine

30

Artist: **Mark Summers**

Art Director: Marti Golon

Client: TIME

Medium: Engraving in scratchboard

31

Artist: **Andrea Ventura**

Art Director: Edel Rodriguez

Client: TIME Latin American Edition

Medium: Mixed on paper

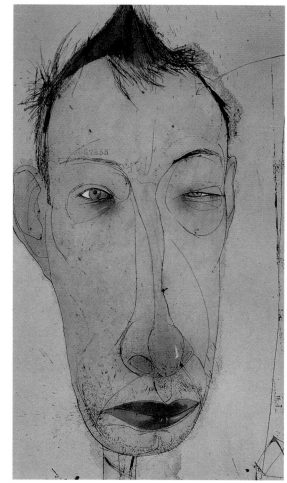

27

28

29

30

31

32

Artist: **Joe Ciardiello**
Art Director: Nancy McMillen
Client: Texas Monthly
Medium: Pen & ink, watercolor on paper
Size: 15" x 9"

33

Artist: **Joe Ciardiello**
Art Director: Tamotsu Ejima
Client: Playboy Japan
Medium: Pen & ink, watercolor on paper
Size: 15" x 12"

34

Artist: **David Johnson**
Art Director: Joe Dizney
Client: The Wall Street Journal
Medium: Pen & ink on paper
Size: 10" x 8"

35

Artist: **Gary Kelley**
Art Director: Deborah Clark
Client: American Spectator
Medium: Pastel on paper
Size: 20" x 14"

36

Artist: **Marshall Arisman**
Art Director: Louise Kollenbaum
Client: California Lawyer
Medium: Oil on paper

Mance Lipscomb

32

J. Edgar Hoover & Friend

33

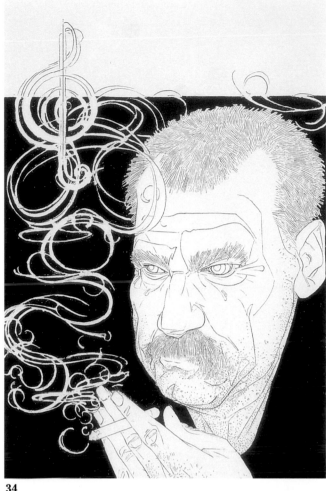

34

35

36

37

Artist: **Tim Bower**

Art Director: Kelly Doe

Client: Washington Post

Medium: Acrylic on paper

Size: 12" x 12"

38

Artist: **Tim Bower**

Art Director: John Boyer

Client: Condé Nast GQ

Medium: Acrylic on paper

Size: 10" x 8"

39

Artist: **Gregory Manchess**

Art Director: Ed Rich

Client: Smithsonian Magazine

Medium: Oil on board

Size: 11" x 36"

40

Artist: **Gregory Manchess**

Art Director: Ed Rich

Client: Smithsonian Magazine

Medium: Oil on board

Size: 21" x 32"

37

38

39

40

41

Artist: **Stacy Innerst**

Client: Pittsburgh Post Gazette

Medium: Acrylic on board

Size: 12" x 10"

42

Artist: **Istvan Banyai**

Art Director: Tom Staebler

Client: Playboy

43

Artist: **Scott Snow**

Client: Bonneville Communications

Medium: Oil

Size: 22" x 28"

44

Artist: **Gerald Dubois**

Art Directors: Judy Garlan,
                Robin Gilmore-Barnes

Client: The Atlantic Monthly

Medium: Acrylic on paper

Size: 6" x 14"

41

42

43

44

45

Artist: **Gary Kelley**
Art Director: Dan Martin
Client: St. Louis Post-Dispatch
Medium: Pastel on paper
Size: 23" x 14"

46

Artist: **Mike Benny**
Art Directors: Tom Staebler, Kerig Pope
Client: Playboy
Medium: Acrylic

47

Artist: **Benoit**
Art Directors: Dirk Barnett, Tom Brown
Client: Travel & Leisure Golf Magazine
Medium: Oil
Size: 14" x 10"

48

Artist: **N. Ascencios**
Art Director: Wesla Weller
Client: LA Magazine
Medium: Oil on canvas

45

46

47

48

49

Artist: **Michael Gibbs**

Art Director: Sarah Clarke Hollander

Client: Mortgage Banking

Medium: Mixed, digital

Size: 16" x 12"

50

Artist: **Gregory Manchess**

Art Director: Cynthia L. Currie

Client: Kiplinger Magazine

Medium: Oil on board

Size: 17" x 20"

51

Artist: **Mike Benny**

Art Director: Greg Breeding

Client: Moody Magazine

Medium: Acrylic

Size: 18" x 14"

52

Artist: **Terry Allen**

Art Directors: John Korpics,
              Geraldine Hessler

Client: Entertainment Weekly

53

Artist: **Michael Paraskevas**

Art Director: Cynthia L. Currie

Client: Kiplinger's Personal
        Finance Magazine

Medium: Acrylic on paper

Size: 20" x 20"

54

Artist: **Yan Nascimbene**

Art Director: Judy Dombrowski

Client: Creative Living

Medium: Ink, watercolor on Arches paper

Size: 8" x 8"

49

50

51

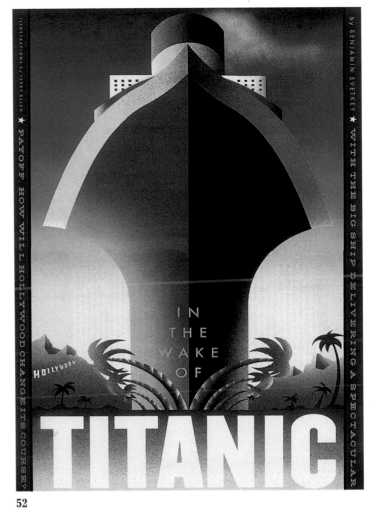

52

53

54

61

Artist: **Peter de Sève**

Art Director: Francoise Mouly

Client: The New Yorker

Medium: Ink, watercolor

Size: 15" x 11"

62

Artist: **Tom Curry**

Art Director: Greg Klee

Client: Natural Health Magazine

Medium: Acrylic on hardboard

Size: 18" x 14"

63

Artist: **William Joyce**

Art Directors: John Korpics,
              Geraldine Hessler

Client: Entertainment Weekly

Medium: Colored pencil on paper

64

Artist: **Joe Sorren**

Art Director: Sue Syrnick

Client: Philadelphia Inquirer

Medium: Acrylic on canvas

Size: 40" x 30"

65

Artist: **Jack Unruh**

Art Director: Sue Conley

Client: Red Herring

Medium: Ink, watercolor on board

Size: 17" x 12"

66

Artist: **Joe Sorren**

Art Director: Cynthia L. Currie

Client: Kiplinger's Personal
        Finance Magazine

Medium: Acrylic on canvas

Size: 30" x 24"

61

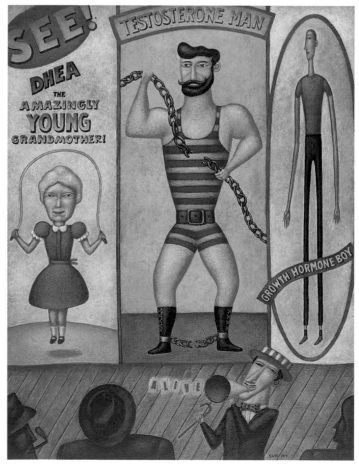

62

63

64

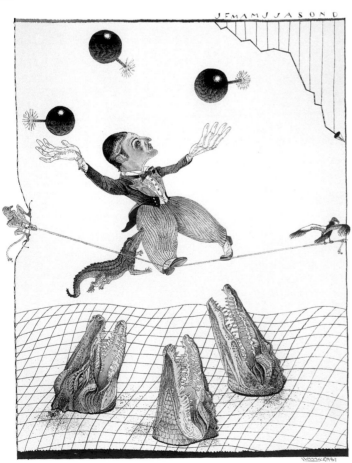

65

66

67

Artist: **Hanoch Piven**

Art Director: John Giordani

Client: Details Magazine

Medium: Mixed, collage

Size: 12" x 9"

68

Artist: **Dugald Stermer**

Art Director: Susan Anderson

Client: Coastal Living Magazine

Medium: Pencil, watercolor on Arches

Size: 20" x 14"

69

Artist: **Brad Holland**

Art Director: Judy Garlan

Client: The Atlantic Monthly

Medium: Acrylic on masonite

Size: 20" x 26"

70

Artist: **Robert Giusti**

Art Director: Lynn Phelps

Client: Utne Reader

Medium: Acrylic on linen

Size: 15" x 12"

67

68

69

70

BOOK

JURY

Barnett Plotkin, Chairman
Illustrator

Bunny Carter
Illustrator/Writer, Professor San Jose State University

Diviya Magaro
Program management, Easton Press

Wm. A. Motta
Art Director/Illustrator

Rafal Olbinski
Illustrator

Jim Pearson
Art Director, Pixar Animation Studios

Bobbi Tull
Illustrator

Kent Williams
Illustrator

71 GOLD MEDAL

Artist: **Laurel Long**

Art Directors: Nancy Leo, Atha Tehon

Client: Dial Books for Young Readers

Medium: Oil on paper

Size: 13" x 21"

Laurel Long's first book, *The Mightiest Heart,* was based on a Welsh legend about a prince and his faithful dog. An Associate Professor of Art at California State University, Northridge, her work is influenced by Early Flemish and 17th century Dutch painting. Through detail and texture characteristic of those periods, she hopes to create a complete world through which characters and readers can travel.

72 GOLD MEDAL

Artist: **Chris Sheban**

Art Director: Rita Marshall

Client: Creative Education

Medium: Graphite, watercolor, pencil on paper

Size: 9" x 19"

"Creative Education sent me a manuscript about a 'barn-tall' plainswoman who, along with her horse, travels the towns of Ohio hand sewing and delivering her 'last-a-lifetime' shoes to the grateful townfolk. Sounded good to me. The story offered many opportunities for images tinged with understated humor."

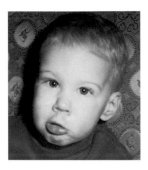

73 SILVER MEDAL

Artist: **Michael Koelsch**

Art Directors: Vaughan Johnson,
Michael Koelsch

Client: Harcourt Brace & Co.

Medium: Acrylic, Prismacolor pencils
on board

Size: 20" x 15"

The artist summed up the story for this illustration in one word: "Bizarre." The book is full of symbolism and the name carved on the wooden board in the background recurs in the text.

74 SILVER MEDAL

Artist: **Gregory Manchess**

Art Director: Nancy Leo

Client: Dial Books for Young Readers

Medium: Oil on linen

Size: 19" x 14"

"This painting is from my second children's book, *Nanuk: Lord of the Ice*. I poured over books about the arctic, polar bears, and sled dogs. I found nothing close to the reference I needed, so I just began drawing. I was apprehensive about starting the finish because I wanted to match the image in my mind. So, after straightening a few shelves, sweeping the deck, and renovating the kitchen, I jumped in. A shaky start and an ugly stage later, it painted itself. The smooth ones always sneak up on you."

75 SILVER MEDAL

Artist: **Jerry Pinkney**

Art Director: Atha Tehon

Client: Dial Books for Young Readers

Medium: Pencil, watercolor, gouache on
Arches watercolor paper

Size: 14" x 22"

"As a young boy growing up in Philadelphia, PA,
I dreamed of exploring the Wild West. I played
cowboys, and with great enthusiasm became the
characters portrayed on the silver screen. Today I
wonder how my role-playing and self-esteem
would have been enhanced had I known about the
number of Black cowboys who were in the ranks
of early American frontiersmen."

76

Artist: **C.F. Payne**

Art Director: Paul Buckley

Client: Penguin Putnam, Inc.

Medium: Mixed on board

Size: 15" x 12"

76

77

Artist: **Ian Schoenherr**

Art Director: Cecilia Yung

Client: Philomel Books

Medium: Oil, acrylic on paper

Size: 16" x 12"

78

Artist: **Shelly Hehenberger**

Art Director: Lucille Chomowicz

Client: Simon & Schuster Books for
Young Readers

Medium: Pastel, colored pencil on paper

Size: 14" x 11"

79

Artist: **Paul Cozzolino**

Art Director: Kathleen Lynch

Client: Oxford University Press

Medium: Oil on board

Size: 14" x 11"

80

Artist: **Doug Chayka**

Art Director: Tim Gillner

Client: Boyds Mills Press

Medium: Oil on canvas

Size: 24" x 18"

81

Artist: **K.W. Popp**

Art Director: Atha Tehon

Client: Dial Books for Young Readers

Medium: Pastel on paper

Size: 17" x 32"

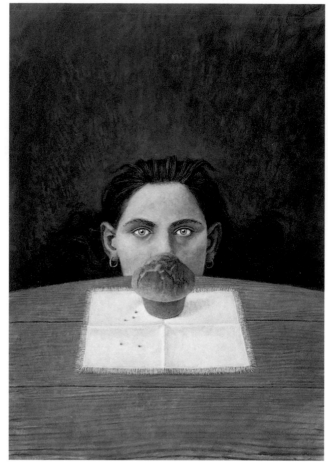

77

78

79

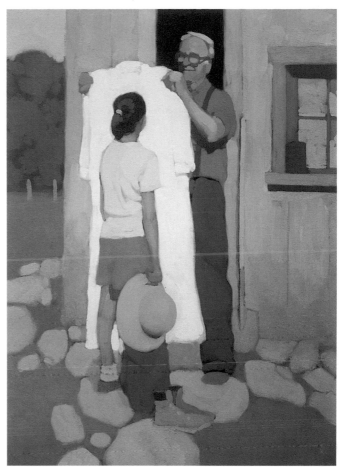

80

81

82

Artist: **Marc Burckhardt**

Art Director: Paolo Pepe

Client: Pocket Books

Medium: Acrylic on cold press

83

Artist: **John Clapp**

Art Directors: Allyn Johnston,
Linda Lockowitz

Client: Harcourt Brace & Co.

Medium: Watercolor over graphite
on paper

Size: 13" x 10"

84

Artist: **John Clapp**

Art Directors: Allyn Johnston,
Linda Lockowitz

Client: Harcourt Brace & Co.

Medium: Watercolor over graphite
drawing on paper

Size: 13" x 10"

85

Artist: **John Jude Palencar**

Art Director: Paul Zakris

Client: Simon & Schuster

Medium: Acrylic on Strathmore

Size: 20" x 15"

86

Artist: **Robert Hunt**

Art Director: John Gibson

Client: Paul Foundation

Medium: Oil on board

Size: 26" x 18"

82

83

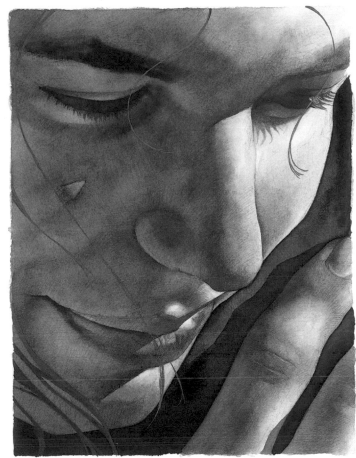

84

85

86

87

Artist: **Yvonne Buchanan**

Art Director: Lucille Chomowicz

Client: Simon & Schuster

Medium: Watercolor on paper

Size: 12" x 18"

88

Artist: **Yvonne Buchanan**

Art Director: Lucille Chomowicz

Client: Simon & Schuster

Medium: Watercolor on paper

Size: 12" x 18"

89

Artist: **K.W. Popp**

Art Director: Atha Tehon

Client: Dial Books for Young Readers

Medium: Pastel on paper

Size: 17" x 32"

90

Artist: **K.W. Popp**

Art Director: Atha Tehon

Client: Dial Books for Young Readers

Medium: Pastel on paper

Size: 17" x 32"

87

88

89

90

91

Artist: **Ken Joudrey**

Art Director: Krista Olson

Client: St. Martin's Press

Medium: Acrylic, oil on gessoed board

Size: 13" x 9"

92

Artist: **Glenn Harrington**

Art Director: Toni Ellis

Client: University of Chicago Press

Medium: Oil on linen

Size: 14" x 20"

93

Artist: **Michael Dooling**

Art Director: Barbara Fitzsimmons

Client: William Morrow Books of Wonder

Medium: Oil on masonite

Size: 18" x 14"

94

Artist: **Kazuhiko Sano**

Art Director: Yook Louie

Client: Bantam Books

Medium: Acrylic on textured board

Size: 25" x 18"

95

Artist: **Michael Koelsch**

Art Director: Paul Elliott

Client: Dreamworks

Medium: Acrylic on board

Size: 20" x 15"

91

92

93

94

95

101

Artist: **Douglas Smith**

Art Director: Leslie Goldman

Client: Little, Brown & Co.

Medium: Scratchboard, watercolor

Size: 15" x 10"

102

Artist: **Joseph Daniel Fiedler**

Art Director: Nina Barnett

Client: Simon & Schuster

Medium: Alkyd on Strathmore Bristol

Size: 13" x 10"

103

Artist: **Joseph Daniel Fiedler**

Art Director: Nina Barnett

Client: Simon & Schuster

Medium: Alkyd on Strathmore Bristol

Size: 13" x 10"

104

Artist: **Joseph Daniel Fiedler**

Art Director: Nina Barnett

Client: Simon & Schuster

Medium: Alkyd on Strathmore Bristol

Size: 13" x 10"

105

Artist: **Albert Lorenz**

Client: Harry N. Abrams

Medium: Mixed on Bristol

Size: 24" x 18"

101

102

103

104

105

106

Artist: **H.B. Lewis**

Art Director: Rita Marshall

Client: Creative Editions

Medium: Pastel on paper

Size: 15" x 13"

107

Artist: **Greg Harlin**

Art Director: Lucille Chomowicz

Client: Simon & Schuster

Medium: Acrylic, gouache, oil on
        illustration board

Size: 12" x 9"

108

Artist: **H.B. Lewis**

Art Director: Rita Marshall

Client: Creative Editions

Medium: Pastel on paper

Size: 13" x 20"

109

Artist: **H.B. Lewis**

Art Director: Rita Marshall

Client: Creative Editions

Medium: Pastel on paper

Size: 13" x 20"

106

107

108

109

110

Artist: **Robert Hunt**

Art Directors: Sharon Collins,
                    Jennifer Spaulding

Client: Thomas Nelson Publishing

Medium: Oil on board

Size: 28" x 20"

111

Artist: **Mark Elliott**

Art Director: Isabel Warren-Lynch

Client: Alfred A. Knopf Paperbacks

Medium: Acrylic on Strathmore board

Size: 14" x 19"

112

Artist: **John Thompson**

Art Directors: Nancy Leo, Atha Tehon

Client: Dial Books for Young Readers

Medium: Acrylic on board

Size: 18" x 24"

113

Artist: **Peter Sis**

Art Director: Lily Rosenstreich

Client: Farrar, Straus & Giroux

Medium: Mixed on paper

Size: 14" x 28"

110

111

112

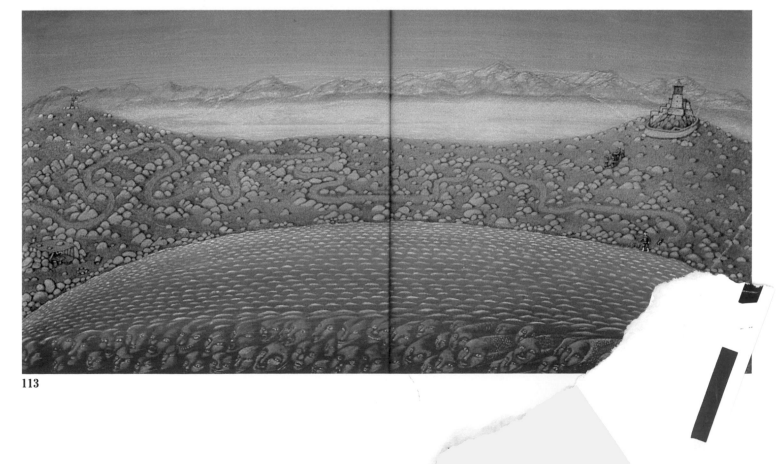

113

114

Artist: **David Slonim**

Art Director: Rudy Ramos

Client: Northland Publishing

Medium: Oil on linen

Size: 11" x 13"

115

Artist: **Dave McKean**

Art Director: Donald Grant Publishing

Medium: Digital

Size: 11" x 9"

116

Artist: **Dan Andreasen**

Art Director: Al Cetta

Client: HarperCollins

Medium: Oil on board

Size: 22" x 36"

117

Artist: **Jerry Pinkney**

Art Director: Atha Tehon

Client: Dial Books for Young Readers

Medium: Pencil, watercolor, gouache on Arches watercolor paper

Size: 15" x 23"

118

Artist: **Jerry Pinkney**

Art Director: Atha Tehon

Client: Dial Books for Young Readers

Medium: Pencil, watercolor, gouache on Arches watercolor paper

Size: 14" x 22"

114

115

116

117

118

119

Artist: **Bernie Fuchs**

Art Directors: Maria Modugno,
Sue Dennen

Client: Little, Brown & Co.

Medium: Oil on canvas

Size: 30" x 21"

120

Artists: **Steve Johnson, Lou Fancher**

Art Director: Lou Fancher

Client: Harcourt Brace & Co.

Medium: Oil, acrylic, fabric on canvas

Size: 16" x 15"

121

Artist: **Bernie Fuchs**

Art Directors: Maria Modugno,
Sue Dennen

Client: Little, Brown & Co.

Medium: Oil on canvas

Size: 24" x 36"

122

Artist: **David Christiana**

Art Directors: Shiela Smallwood,
Maria Modugno

Client: Little, Brown & Co.

Medium: Watercolor on paper

Size: 10" x 20"

123

Artist: **David Christiana**

Art Directors: Shiela Smallwood,
Maria Modugno

Client: Little, Brown & Co.

Medium: Watercolor on paper

Size: 10" x 20"

119

120

121

122

123

124

Artist: **E.B. Lewis**

Art Director: Atha Tehon

Client: Dial Books for Young Readers

Medium: Watercolor on paper

Size: 9" x 11"

125

Artist: **Joe Morse**

Art Director: Alan Michael Parker

Client: Boa Editions

Medium: Oil, acrylic on paper

Size: 15" x 11"

126

Artist: **Jon J. Muth**

Art Director: Robbin Brosterman

Client: DC/Vertigo Comics

Medium: Watercolor on paper

Size: 10" x 8"

127

Artist: **Jon J. Muth**

Art Director: Robbin Brosterman

Client: DC/Vertigo Comics

Medium: Watercolor on paper

Size: 10" x 8"

128

Artist: **Jon J. Muth**

Art Director: Robbin Brosterman

Client: DC/Vertigo Comics

Medium: Watercolor on paper

Size: 15" x 11"

129

Artist: **Gary Kelley**

Art Director: Rita Marshall

Client: Creative Editions

Medium: Pastel on paper

Size: 18" x 13"

124

125

126

127

128

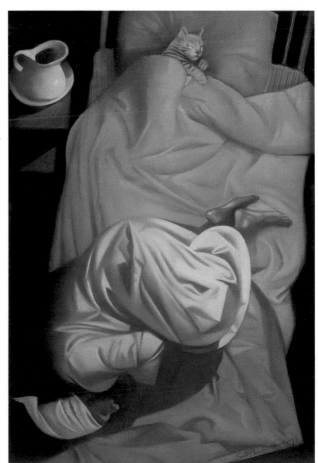

129

130

Artist: **Peter de Sève**

Art Director: Roseanne Serra

Client: Penguin USA

Medium: Watercolor on watercolor paper

Size: 15" x 10"

131

Artist: **Peter de Sève**

Art Directors: Michael Farmer,
                Michael Stearns

Client: Harcourt Brace & Co.

Medium: Watercolor on watercolor paper

Size: 15" x 10"

132

Artist: **Daniel Adel**

Art Director: Michael Farmer

Client: Harcourt Brace & Co.

Medium: Oil on board

133

Artist: **Cathleen Toelke**

Art Director: Gail Dubov

Client: Avon Books

Medium: Gouache on watercolor board

Size: 9" x 8"

134

Artist: **Leonid Gore**

Art Director: Chris Hamill Paul

Client: DK Ink

Medium: Acrylic on paper

Size: 18" x 13"

135

Artist: **Cathleen Toelke**

Art Director: Gail Dubov

Client: Avon Books

Medium: Gouache on watercolor board

Size: 9" x 8"

130

131

132

133

134

135

136

Artist: **John Rush**

Art Director: Audrey Niffenegger

Client: The Shadow Press

Medium: Copper plate etching
      on Rives BFK

Size: 12" x 9"

137

Artist: **Kinuko Y. Craft**

Art Director: Paolo Pepe

Client: Simon & Schuster

Medium: Oil, watercolor on board

Size: 18" x 18"

138

Artist: **Glenn Harrington**

Art Director: Jim Plumeri

Client: Bantam Books

Medium: Oil on rag board

Size: 26" x 18"

139

Artist: **Hiro Kimura**

Art Director: Jill Bossert

Client: Society of Illustrators

Medium: Acrylic on board

Size: 14" x 10"

140

Artist: **Thom Ang**

Art Director: David Stevenson

Client: The Ballantine Publishing Group

Medium: Mixed, digital

Size: 9" x 13"

141

Artist: **Rafal Olbinski**

Art Director: Elizabeth Parisi

Client: Scholastic Press

Medium: Oil on board

Size: 36" x 24"

136

137

138

139

140

141

142

Artist: **John Jude Palencar**

Art Director: Donald Puckey

Client: Warner Books

Medium: Acrylic on panel

Size: 12" x 12"

143

Artist: **Scott Swales**

Art Director: Jacqueline Cooke

Client: Prometheus Books

Medium: Pastel, acrylic on paper

Size: 13" x 10"

144

Artist: **Thom Ang**

Art Director: Richard Thomas

Client: White Wolf Publishing

Medium: Mixed, digital

Size: 6" x 4"

145

Artist: **Dave McKean**

Client: Allen Spiegel Fine Arts/Hourglass

Medium: Digital

Size: 24" x 24"

146

Artist: **Cliff Nielsen**

Art Director: Joanna Cotler

Client: HarperCollins

Medium: Digital

Size: 20" x 15"

147

Artist: **Dave McKean**

Client: Allen Spiegel Fine Arts/Hourglass

Medium: Digital

Size: 24" x 24"

142

143

144

145

146

147

148

Artist: **Wendell Minor**

Art Director: Michael Farmer

Client: BrownDeer Press

Medium: Watercolor on board

Size: 9" x 12"

149

Artist: **Leonid Gore**

Art Director: David Saylor

Client: Scholastic Press

Medium: Acrylic on paper

Size: 11" x 11"

150

Artist: **John Jude Palencar**

Art Director: David Stevenson

Client: Del Rey/Ballantine Books

Medium: Acrylic on ragboard

Size: 19" x 40"

151

Artist: **Omaha Perez**

Client: Slave Labor

Medium: Acrylic, ink on paper

Size: 16" x 11"

152

Artist: **Tristan Elwell**

Art Director: Liney Li

Client: Bantam Doubleday Dell

Medium: Oil on masonite

Size: 18" x 12"

148

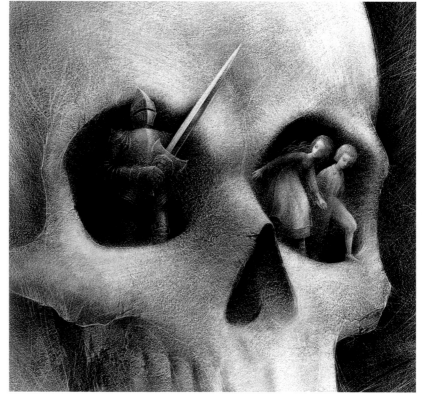

149

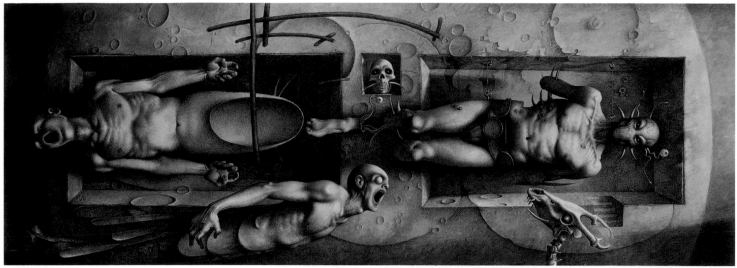

150

151

152

153
Artist: **Marshall Arisman**
Client: Vanguard Studio
Medium: Oil on paper
Size: 29" x 22"

154
Artist: **Cliff Nielsen**
Art Director: Vicki Sheatsly
Client: Bantam Books
Medium: Digital
Size: 20" x 10"

155
Artist: **Bruce Waldman**
Art Director: Wendy Halitzer
Client: Grove Press Books
Medium: Monoprint on paper
Size: 24" x 30"

156
Artist: **Cliff Nielsen**
Art Director: Vicki Sheatsly
Client: Bantam Books
Medium: Digital
Size: 20" x 10"

157
Artist: **Tim O'Brien**
Art Directors: Tom Egner, Gail Dubov
Client: Avon Books
Medium: Oil on board
Size: 16" x 12"

153

154

155

156

157

158

Artist: **Edward Miller**

Art Director: Alison Williams

Client: Tor Books

Medium: Oil on canvas board

159

Artist: **Raúl Colón**

Art Director: Chris Hammill Paul

Client: Orchard Books

Medium: Watercolor, colored pencil on
watercolor paper

160

Artist: **Donato Giancola**

Art Director: Irene Gallo

Client: Tor Books

Medium: Oil on paper on masonite

Size: 22" x 34"

161

Artist: **Raúl Colón**

Art Director: Chris Hammill Paul

Client: Orchard Books

Medium: Watercolor, colored pencil on
watercolor paper

158

159

160

161

162

Artist: **Michael Garland**

Art Director: Amy Shields

Client: The Millbrook Press

Medium: Mixed, pencil, digital on paper

163

Artist: **Vincent Di Fate**

Art Director: Irene Gallo

Client: Tor Books

Medium: Acrylic on hardboard

Size: 15" x 20"

164

Artist: **Michael Garland**

Art Director: Amy Shields

Client: The Millbrook Press

Medium: Mixed, pencil, digital on paper

165

Artist: **Kinuko Y. Craft**

Art Director: Judith Murello

Client: Berkley Books

Medium: Oil, watercolor on board

Size: 16" x 12"

166

Artist: **Tomas Canty**

Art Director: Irene Gallo

Client: Tor Books

Medium: Oil on paper

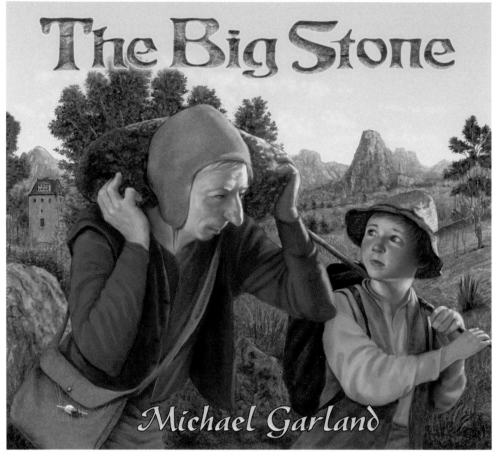

162

163

164

165

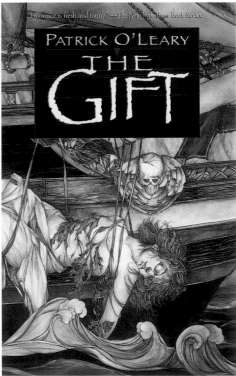

166

167

Artist: **Kam Mak**

Art Director: Al Cetta

Client: HarperCollins

Medium: Oil on masonite

Size: 14" x 11"

168

Artist: **Kam Mak**

Art Director: Al Cetta

Client: HarperCollins

Medium: Oil on masonite

Size: 12" x 10"

169

Artist: **David Christiana**

Art Directors: Shiela Smallwood,
Maria Modugno

Client: Little, Brown & Co.

Medium: Watercolor on paper

Size: 10" x 20"

170

Artist: **Lori Lohstoeter**

Art Director: Anne Davies

Client: Harcourt Brace & Co.

Medium: Acrylic on board

Size: 15" x 20"

167

168

169

170

171

Artist: **Mark Riedy**

Art Director: Nancy Gonzalez

Client: Workman Publishing

Medium: Digital

Size: 9" x 11"

172

Artist: **Mark Riedy**

Art Director: Nancy Gonzalez

Client: Workman Publishing

Medium: Digital

Size: 9" x 11"

173

Artist: **David Shannon**

Art Director: Kathleen Westray

Client: Blue Sky Press

Medium: Acrylic, Prismacolor on board

Size: 11" x 17"

174

Artist: **David Shannon**

Art Director: Kathleen Westray

Client: Blue Sky Press

Medium: Acrylic, Prismacolor on board

Size: 11" x 17"

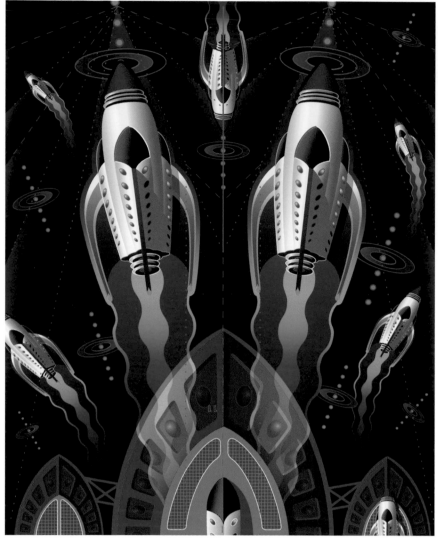

171

172

173

174

180

Artist: **Carter Goodrich**

Client: Harcourt Brace & Co.

Medium: Colored pencil, watercolor on watercolor board

Size: 17" x 12"

181

Artist: **Paul Yalowitz**

Art Director: Sarah Caguiat

Client: Orchard Books

Medium: Colored pencil on Bristol vellum paper

Size: 9" x 6"

182

Artist: **David Shannon**

Art Director: Kathleen Westray

Client: Blue Sky Press

Medium: Acrylic, Prismacolor on board

Size: 11" x 17"

183

Artist: **Joan Steiner**

Client: Little, Brown & Co.

Medium: Mixed, found objects

180

181

182

183

184

Artist: **John Backlund**

Art Director: Judy Turziano

Client: The Greenwich Workshop Press

Medium: Watercolor on paper

Size: 20" x 30"

185

Artists: **Steve Johnson, Lou Fancher**

Art Director: Lou Fancher

Client: Hyperion Books/Disney Press

Medium: Oil on paper

Size: 14" x 12"

186

Artist: **Joan Steiner**

Client: Little, Brown & Co.

Medium: Mixed, found objects

Size: 24" x 40" x 18"

187

Artist: **Martin Matje**

Art Directors: Martha Rego,
Christy Ottaviano

Client: Henry Holt & Company

Medium: Gouache on paper

Size: 15" x 30"

184

185

186

187

188

Artist: **John Clapp**

Art Directors: Allyn Johnston,
Linda Lockowitz

Client: Harcourt Brace & Co.

Medium: Watercolor over graphite
drawing on paper

Size: 13" x 10"

189

Artist: **Tim Jonke**

Art Director: Andrea Boven

Client: Charlot/Victor

Medium: Oil on 2-ply Strathmore

Size: 10" x 16"

190

Artist: **Greg Newbold**

Art Director: Linda Zuckerman

Client: BrownDeer Press

Medium: Acrylic on Bristol

Size: 10" x 20"

191

Artist: **Greg Newbold**

Art Director: Linda Zuckerman

Client: BrownDeer Press

Medium: Acrylic on Bristol

Size: 10" x 20"

188

189

190

191

192

Artist: **John Sandford**

Client: Lothrop, Lee & Shepard Books

Medium: Watercolor on peat moss
imbedded paper

Size: 15" x 15"

193

Artist: **Charles Santore**

Art Directors: Cathy Goldsmith,
Cathy Bobak

Client: Random House

Medium: Watercolor on Arches
90 lb. paper

Size: 6" x 10"

194

Artist: **Charles Santore**

Art Directors: Cathy Goldsmith,
Cathy Bobak

Client: Random House

Medium: Watercolor on Arches
90 lb. paper

Size: 6" x 10"

195

Artist: **Charles Santore**

Art Directors: Cathy Goldsmith,
Cathy Bobak

Client: Random House

Medium: Watercolor on Arches
90 lb. paper

Size: 6" x 10"

196

Artist: **Don Daily**

Art Director: Frances J. Soo Ping Chow

Client: Running Press

Medium: Watercolor on Arches

Size: 21" X 11"

192

193

194

195

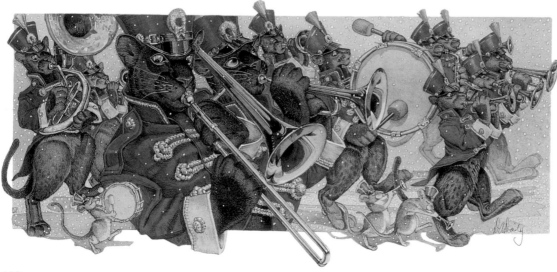

196

208

Artist: **Bernie Fuchs**

Art Directors: Maria Modugno,
 Sue Dennen

Client: Little, Brown & Co.

Medium: Oil on canvas

Size: 33" x 24"

209

Artist: **Michael Garland**

Art Director: Tim Gillner

Client: Boyds Mills Press

Medium: Mixed, pencil, digital on paper

Size: 10" x 11"

208

209

ADVERTISING

JURY

Jacqui Morgan, Chairman
Illustrator/Painter/Author

Sally Wern Comport
Illustrator

David DeVries
Illustrator

Bruce Jensen
Illustrator

Lucinda Levine
Illustrator

Doreen Minuto
Illustrator

David J. Passalacqua
Illustrator/Photographer/Teacher

Simms Taback
Illustrator

Bertram Ulrich
Curator, NASA Art Program

210 GOLD MEDAL

Artist: **Loren Long**

Client: American Heart Association

Medium: Acrylic on board

Size: 26" x 15"

"Year after year, John Maggard delivered beautiful artwork for this much-anticipated poster for the Cincinnati Heart Mini Marathon. With the Cincinnati illustrators being such a friendly bunch, John, overbooked with work, asked me to take on the project for its 21st running. Flattered, my excitement turned into nervous anxiety when someone suggested that it was as if I were pinch-hitting for Lou Gehrig. Buried by the excruciating pressure of the situation, I managed to escape by falling back on the one sure bet that we can all count on—man's best friend. Thank you for this honor."

211 GOLD MEDAL

Artist: **Stephen T. Johnson**

Art Director: David Hadley

Client: KSK Communications/Zebra
Technologies

Medium: Pastel, watercolor on paper

Size: 22" x 17"

The artist has parlayed his *Alphabet City* book nicely. It was from his letter "T" in a previous Annual that KSK Communications contacted him for this print ad for Zebra Technologies. The street here may look random but it has elements of West 24th Street looking towards Sixth Avenue. The job was a rush as well, after an attempt by the client to use photography had failed.

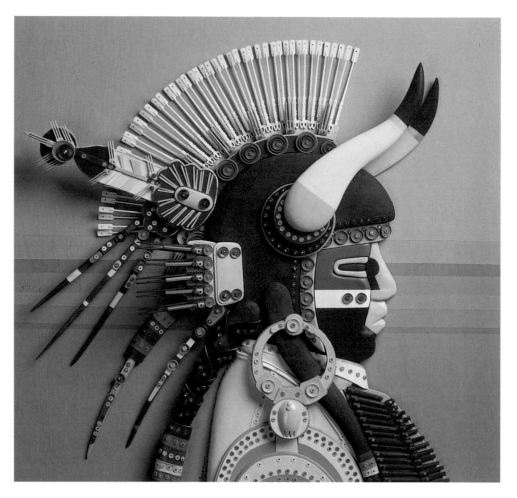

215 SILVER MEDAL

Artist: **Eugene Hoffman**

Client: The Pressworks/Denver

Medium: Mixed, wood, plastic

Size: 38" x 30" x 2"

"Ascribing spiritual meaning to non-human forms is as enduring as is humankind. Attempts to evoke the spirits by making magic through music, masks, costumes, designs and art are as alive today as they were many mysteries ago. The muse's affinity with the 'medium,' whether stone, wood, cloth, paint (or paper and ink), kindles, summons and incites the spirits to dance their magic, albeit fleetingly, and while the images abide, forges our links to them."

216

Artist: **Brad Holland**

Client: Long Wharf Theater

Medium: Acrylic on masonite

216

217

218

217

Artist: **Brad Holland**

Art Director: Jeoff Shirley

Client: AEtna - US Healthcare

Medium: Acrylic on board

218

Artist: **Dave Cutler**

Art Director: Ken Elkinson

Client: Ken Elkinson

Medium: Acrylic, pencils on watercolor paper

223

Artist: **Michael Paraskevas**

Client: Paraskevas Gallery/Storyopolis

Medium: Acrylic on paper

Size: 40" x 30"

224

Artist: **Joe Sorren**

Art Director: Jeff Bartel

Client: Morrow Snowboards

Medium: Acrylic on canvas

Size: 48" x 15"

225

Artist: **Don Weller**

Client: Park City Lodestar

Medium: Digital

Size: 20" x 15"

226

Artist: **W.C. Burgard**

Art Directors: Colleen Murdock,
                Mary Oleniczak

Client: Ann Arbor Summer Festival

Medium: Collage on plywood

Size: 8" x 25"

223

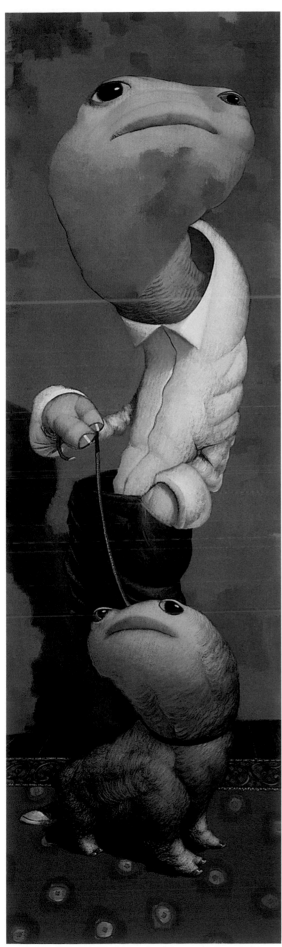

224

225

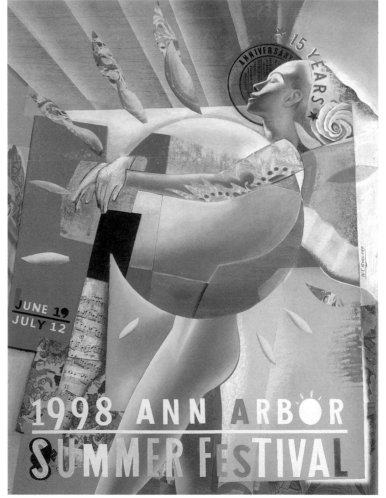

226

227

Artist: **Rafal Olbinski**

Client: Danuta Foundation

Medium: Oil on canvas

Size: 30" x 20"

228

Artist: **Steven Adler**

Art Director: David Coleman

Client: Sony Music

Medium: Oil on Bristol board

Size: 12" x 9"

229

Artist: **Barbara Nessim**

Art Director: Maia Muller

Client: Carlson & Partners

Medium: Brush & ink scanned into
Photoshop (Iris Print)

Size: 17" x 11"

230

Artist: **Jody Hewgill**

Art Director: Scott Mires

Client: Arena Stage

Medium: Acrylic on board

Size: 18" x 12"

231

Artist: **Gregory Manchess**

Client: Witham Gallery

Medium: Oil on linen

Size: 24" x 19"

232

Artist: **Jody Hewgill**

Art Director: Scott Mires

Client: Arena Stage

Medium: Acrylic on board

Size: 18" x 12"

227

228

229

230

231

232

256

Artist: **Kadir Nelson**

Art Director: Al Jones

Client: Polygram Group Distribution

Medium: Oil on canvas

Size: 24" x 24"

257

Artist: **Fletcher Sibthorp**

Art Director: Connie Gage

Client: Narada Productions, Ltd.

Medium: Mixed

258

Artist: **Raúl Colón**

Art Director: Brian Cubarney

Client: Banco Popular

Medium: Watercolor, colored pencil on
    watercolor paper

259

Artist: **Linda Fennimore**

Art Director: Frank Verlizzo

Client: Hallmark Entertainment

Medium: Colored pencil on paper

Size: 21" x 13"

260

Artist: **Glenn Harrington**

Art Director: Jim Plumeri

Client: Bantam Doubleday Dell

Medium: Oil on board

Size: 28" x 18"

261

Artist: **Greg Newbold**

Art Director: Josh Jenkins

Client: Utah Opera

Medium: Acrylic on Strathmore

Size: 10" x 10"

256

257

258

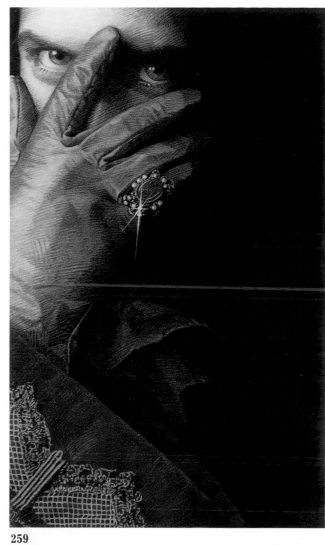

259

260

261

262

Artist: **David Grove**

Art Director: Phil Bauer

Client: Custom Chrome

Medium: Gouache, acrylic

Size: 24" x 16"

263

Artist: **Joyce Patti**

Art Director: Jim Plumeri

Client: BBC (Audio Division)

Medium: Oil on board

Size: 18" x 11"

264

Artist: **Victor Stabin**

Art Director: Roger Musich

Client: Klemtner

Medium: Digital

265

Artist: **Victor Stabin**

Art Director: Roger Musich

Client: Klemtner

Medium: Digital

262

263

264

265

266

Artist: **Kinuko Y. Craft**

Art Director: Kathleen Ryan

Client: Dallas Opera

Medium: Mixed on board

Size: 30" x 24"

267

Artist: **Kazuhiko Sano**

Art Director: Anilda Ward

Client: Telarc International

Medium: Acrylic on masonite

Size: 17" x 17"

268

Artist: **Vivienne Flesher**

Art Director: Ty Cumbie

Client: Lincoln Center

Medium: Pastel on paper

Size: 20" x 16"

269

Artist: **Christopher Peterson**

Art Director: Arlene Owseichik

Client: Bill Graham Presents

Medium: Acrylic on board

Size: 19" x 13"

270

Artist: **Kadir Nelson**

Art Director: D.L. Warfield

Client: La Face Records

Medium: Oil on canvas

Size: 22" x 22"

266

267

268

269

270

275

Artist: **Bill Nelson**

Client: Virginia Commonwealth
University

Medium: Colored pencil on matte board

Size: 30" x 10"

276

Artist: **Steve Brodner**

Art Director: Warren Beatty

Client: 20th Century Fox

Medium: Watercolor on watercolor paper

Size: 20" x 15"

277

Artist: **Bill Mayer**

Art Director: Eric Kessel

Client: Tour De France

Medium: Dyes, gouache, airbrush on
hot press board

Size: 15" x 10"

278

Artist: **Bill Mayer**

Art Director: Dave Helfrey

Client: Lightware Inc.

Medium: Dyes, gouache, airbrush on
hot press board

Size: 5" x 10"

279

Artist: **Bill Mayer**

Art Director: Eric Kessel

Client: Tour De France

Medium: Dyes, gouache, airbrush on
hot press board

Size: 15" x 10"

275

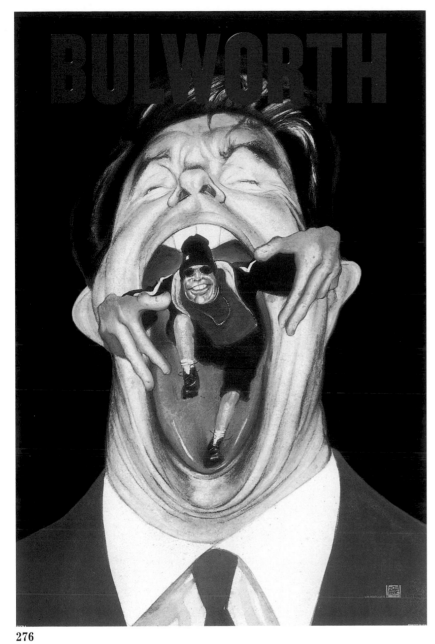

276

277

278

279

280

Artist: **Mark Summers**

Art Directors: George Vogt, Jef Loeb

Client: Yale New Haven Health

Medium: Scratchboard

Size: 12" x 12"

281

Artist: **Mark Summers**

Art Directors: George Vogt, Jef Loeb

Client: Yale New Haven Health

Medium: Scratchboard

Size: 14" x 11"

282

Artist: **Mark Summers**

Art Directors: George Vogt, Jef Loeb

Client: Yale New Haven Health

Medium: Scratchboard

Size: 10" x 10"

283

Artist: **Dugald Stermer**

Art Director: Michael Osborne

Client: The Wine Alliance

Medium: Pencil, watercolor on Arches

284

Artist: **Luba Lukova**

Art Director: Andrei Serban

Client: Columbia University Theatre Division

Medium: Silkscreen on paper

Size: 30" x 20"

280

281

282

283

284

285

Artist: **Susan M. Blubaugh**

Art Director: Maria Kerdel

Client: Ken Wessel

Medium: Watercolor, gouache on paper

Size: 7" x 7"

286

Artist: **Braldt Bralds**

Art Directors: Frank Stovall, Braldt Bralds

Client: Canandaigua Wine Co.

Medium: Oil on canvas

Size: 18" x 18"

287

Artist: **Gary Overacre**

Art Director: David Bartels

Client: Long Island Fine Arts Council

Medium: Oil

Size: 14" x 36"

288

Artist: **David Lance Goines**

Client: Chez Panisse Foundation

Medium: Photo-offset lithography

Size: 24" x 18"

289

Artist: **David Lance Goines**

Client: Chez Panisse Foundation

Medium: Photo-offset lithography

Size: 24" x 18"

285

286

287

288

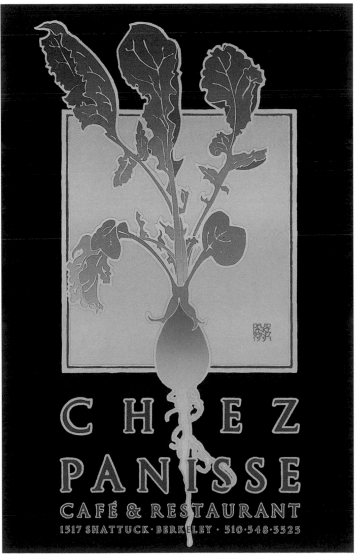

289

290

Artist: **John P. Maggard III**

Client: Greater Cincinnati Chamber of
Commerce

Medium: Acrylic on Strathmore 240

Size: 20" x 15"

291

Artist: **Wilson McLean**

Art Directors: Judy Turziano, Peter Landa

Client: The Greenwich Workshop Press

Medium: Oil on canvas

Size: 22" x 16"

292

Artist: **Chris Sheban**

Art Director: Michael Ridel

Client: Land's End

Medium: Watercolor, pencil on paper

Size: 16" x 13"

293

Artist: **John Sandford**

Client: Lothrop, Lee & Shepard Books

Medium: Watercolor on peat moss
imbedded paper

Size: 16" x 25"

291

292

293

294

Artist: **John C. Berkey**

Art Director: Preston Palmer

Client: GT Interactive Software

Medium: Casein acrylic on board

Size: 18" x 24"

295

Artist: **John C. Berkey**

Art Director: Toby Swartz

Client: Doubleday Science Fiction
Book Club

Medium: Casein acrylic on board

Size: 21" x 16"

294

295

INSTITUTIONAL

JURY

Steve Brodner, Chairman
Illustrator

Robert M. Cunningham
Illustrator

Michael T. Dooling
Children's Book Illustrator

James Gurney
Illustrator

Norman Hotz
Executive Art Editor, Reader's Digest Magazine

Frances Jetter
Illustrator

Steve McCracken
Illustrator

Francoise Mouly
The New Yorker

Brian Pinkney
Illustrator

296 GOLD MEDAL

Artist: **David Johnson**

Art Director: Richard Solomon

Client: Richard Solomon Artists Rep.

Medium: Pen & ink on paper

Size: 24" x 20"

An avid reader, David Johnson chose a passage from P.G. Wodehouse's Jeeves series to illustrate. The setting is London's Drones Club. Aside from corporate executives, dead British authors are Johnson's frequent subjects for *The New York Times Book Review*.

297 GOLD MEDAL

Artist: **Rudy Gutierrez**

Client: Venus Rising Inc.

Medium: Acrylic on table

Size: 48" x 29"

In a recent exhibition, Rudy Gutierrez's art was described as "Wall Medicine." Believing the highest honor is to inspire others, he teaches at Pratt and Parsons. He says, "It is gratifying for 'Night Blossom' to be acknowledged, for it deals with the feeling of anonymity and the flowering which occurs when no one is apparently watching. Painted on a table that was pulled out of the garbage, it proves there's gold to be found where you least expect it." This painting is dedicated to his mother Elsie Detres Gutierrez, a "Night Blossom" if ever there was one.

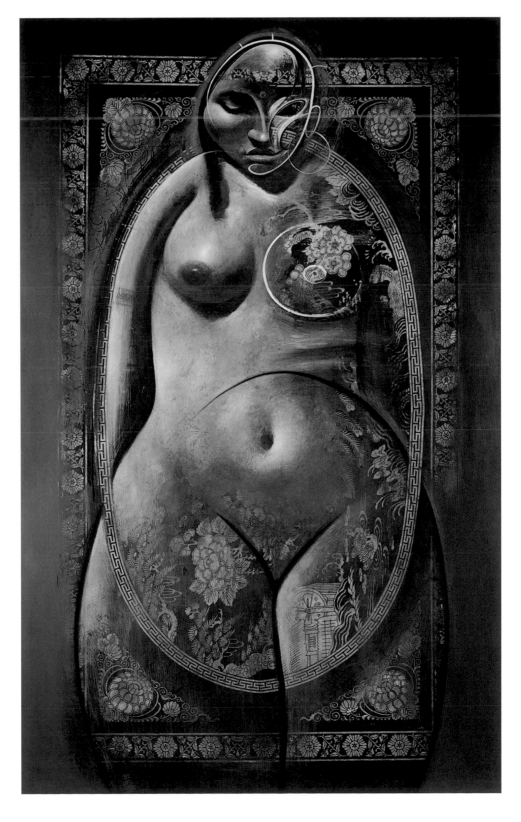

310

Artist: **Brad Holland**

Art Director: Bill Healey

Client: Zanders Ikono Paper Company

Medium: Acrylic on masonite

311

Artist: **Marco Ventura**

Art Director: Neill Roan

Client: Arena Stage

Medium: Oil on paper

Size: 15" x 9"

312

Artist: **Barry Fitzgerald**

Medium: Acrylic on paper

Size: 10" x 11"

313

Artist: **Nicholas Gaetano**

Art Director: Phil Jordan

Client: U.S. Postal Service

Medium: Acrylic on paper

Size: 11" x 7"

314

Artist: **Jay Parnell**

Art Director: Dominic Jannazzo

Medium: Watercolor, pencil on Bristol

Size: 15" x 12"

310

311

312

313

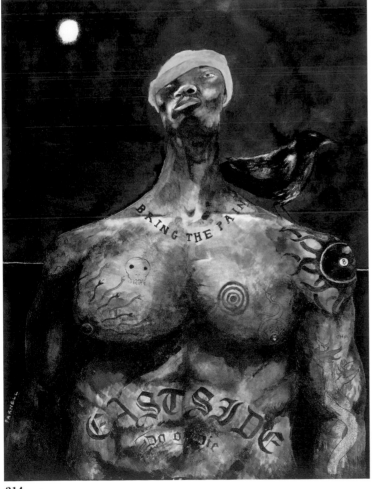

314

321

Artist: **Michael Gibbs**

Client: Illustrators Club of Washington, Maryland & Virgina

Medium: Mixed, digital

Size: 16" x 8"

322

Artist: **Allen Garns**

Art Director: Ted Nuttall

Client: Nuttall Design

Medium: Oil on canvas

Size: 22" x 14"

323

Artist: **Michael Gibbs**

Art Director: Chris Paul

Client: Greenfield-Belser, Inc.

Medium: Mixed, digital

Size: 14" x 11"

324

Artist: **Martin French**

Art Director: Barbara Tyler

Client: Big Brothers of America

Medium: Digital

Size: 23" x 15"

325

Artist: **Martin French**

Art Director: Beth Rielley

Client: Hope International

Medium: Digital

Size: 24" x 18"

321

322

323

324

325

331

Artist: **Bernie Fuchs**
Art Director: Cy Decosse
Client: Interlachen Country Club
Medium: Oil on canvas
Size: 25" x 36"

332

Artist: **Ellen Thompson**
Medium: Watercolor on paper
Size: 14" x 11"

333

Artist: **Gary Kelley**
Art Director: Suzanne Gulbin
Client: National Basketball Association
Medium: Pastel on paper
Size: 30" x 15"

334

Artist: **Mike Benny**
Art Director: Bob Beyn
Client: Seraphein Beyn
Medium: Acrylic
Size: 24" x 18"

335

Artist: **Gary Locke**
Art Director: Ralph Kaufer
Client: Core America
Medium: Watercolor on watercolor board
Size: 14" x 18"

336

Artist: **Ron Mazellan**
Art Director: Joe Ragont
Client: Ragont 2 Design
Medium: Acrylic on paper
Size: 24" x 20"

331

332

333

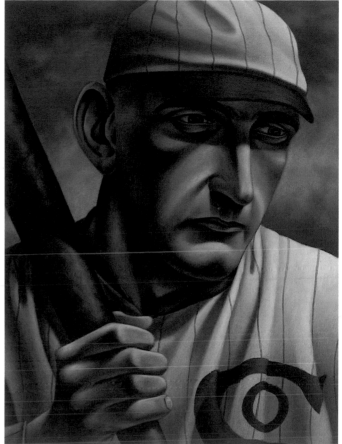

334

335

336

369

Artist: **N. Ascencios**

Client: Algonquin Hotel/Camberly Hotels

Medium: Oil on canvas

Size: 40" x 60"

370

Artist: **Jennie Yip**

Art Director: Stanley D. Hardwick

Client: Flair Communications Agency Inc.

Medium: Gouache on paper

Size: 12" x 18"

371

Artist: **Gary Kelley**

Art Director: Val Paul Taylor

Client: Union Square Grill - Seattle

Medium: Pastel on paper

Size: 14" x 32"

372

Artist: **Gary Aagaard**

Art Directors: Dena Rubin,
                Mordechai Friedman

Client: Ghana Posts and Telecommunications

Medium: Oil on canvas

Size: 8" x 6"

373

Artist: **Gary Aagaard**

Art Director: Dena Rubin

Client: Ghana Posts and Telecommunications

Medium: Oil on canvas

Size: 8" x 6"

369

370

371

372

373

380

Artist: **Jack Unruh**

Art Director: Patrick Short

Client: Asheville

Medium: Ink, watercolor on board

Size: 20" x 11"

381

Artist: **Jack Unruh**

Art Director: Patrick Short

Client: Asheville

Medium: Ink, watercolor on board

Size: 20" x 11"

382

Artist: **Jack Unruh**

Art Director: Patrick Short

Client: Asheville

Medium: Ink, watercolor on board

Size: 20" x 11"

383

Artist: **William Bramhall**

Medium: Pen & ink on paper

384

Artist: **William Bramhall**

Medium: Pen & ink on paper

385

Artist: **William Bramhall**

Medium: Pen & ink on paper

380

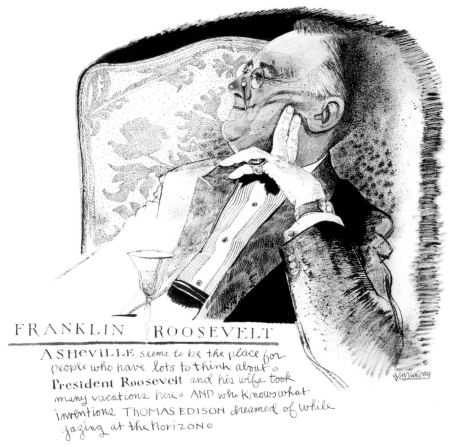

381

F. SCOTT FiTZGERALD

STAY iN RooM 441 of the GROVE PARK inn, and you may find yourself dreaming of JAZZ Bands and swirling parties hosted by A man named GATSBY. Author F. SCOTt FitZGERALD did much of his writing here, and loved the cool mountain energy of ASHEVILLE.

382

383

384

385

386

Artist: **Mark Summers**

Art Director: Richard Solomon

Client: Richard Solomon Artists Rep.

Medium: Scratchboard with overlay

387

Artist: **David Johnson**

Art Director: Richard Solomon

Client: Richard Solomon Artists Rep.

Medium: Pen & ink on paper

Size: 24" x 20"

388

Artist: **John S. Cuneo**

Medium: Acrylic on paper

Size: 9" x 7"

389

Artist: **Murray Tinkelman**

Medium: Pen & ink on Bristol

Size: 16" x 20"

390

Artist: **John S. Cuneo**

Medium: Acrylic on paper

Size: 9" x 7"

391

Artist: **Murray Tinkelman**

Medium: Pen & ink on Bristol

Size: 16" x 20"

392

Artist: **John S. Cuneo**

Medium: Acrylic on paper

Size: 12" x 9"

386

387

388

389

390

391

392

399

Artist: **Laurie Luczak**

Client: American Showcase

Medium: Acrylic, collage on ragboard

Size: 30" x 24"

400

Artist: **Joanne L. Scribner**

Art Director: Isabel Warren Lynch

Client: American Showcase

Medium: Acrylic, ink

Size: 11" x 9"

401

Artist: **Carlos Torres**

Medium: Acrylic on board

18" x 12"

402

Artist: **David O'Keefe**

Client: American Showcase

Medium: Clay, mixed

Size: 12" x 18"

403

Artist: **David O'Keefe**

Client: American Showcase

Medium: Clay, mixed

Size: 18" x 18"

404

Artist: **Mike Liddy**

Medium: Mixed on paper

Size: 14" x 11"

399

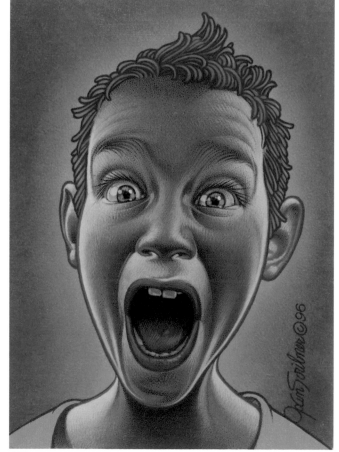

400

401

402

403

404

405

Artist: **Tim Bower**

Art Director: Alyson Boxman

Client: Smoke Magazine

Medium: Acrylic on paper

Size: 10" x 14"

406

Artist: **Jeffrey Smith**

Medium: Watercolor on Lanaquarelle

Size: 12" x 9"

407

Artist: **Teresa Fasolino**

Art Director: Jill Bossert

Client: The Newborn Group

Medium: Oil on canvas glued to masonite

Size: 13" x 12"

408

Artist: **David Bowers**

Medium: Oil on masonite

Size: 14" x 9"

409

Artist: **Michelle Chang**

Medium: Oil on board

Size: 14" x 14"

410

Artist: **Michelle Chang**

Medium: Oil on board

Size: 19" x 15"

405

406

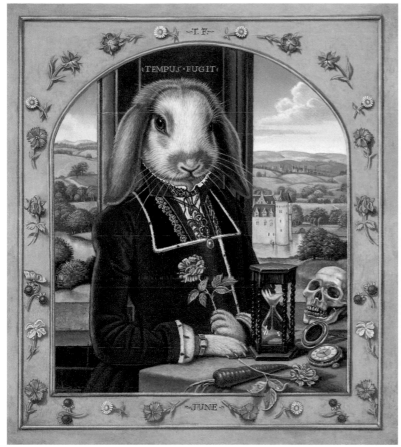

407

408

409

410

417

Artist: **Donato Giancola**

Art Director: Jesper Myrfors

Client: Wizards of the Coast

Medium: Oil on paper on masonite

Size: 8" x 14"

418

Artist: **Donato Giancola**

Art Director: Sue Ann Harkey

Client: Wizards of the Coast

Medium: Oil on paper on masonite

Size: 8" x 10"

419

Artist: **Donato Giancola**

Art Director: Christian Moore

Client: Last Unicorn Games

Medium: Oil on paper on masonite

Size: 7" x 15"

420

Artist: **Scott Snow**

Art Director: Erastus Snow

Client: Family Organization

Medium: Oil on canvas

Size: 48" x 36"

421

Artist: **John Rush**

Art Director: Dr. Maria Hibbs

Client: N.I.P.S.C.O. Industries, Inc.

Medium: Oil on canvas

Size: 28" x 22"

417

418

419

420

421

428

Artist: **Robert Rayevsky**

Client: Salzman International

Medium: Mixed on board

Size: 12" x 9"

429

Artist: **Etienne Delessert**

Art Director: Kathy St. Denny

Client: Xavier Magazine

430

Artist: **Sue Rother**

Client: Tumbleweed Press

Medium: Watercolor on board

Size: 17" x 14"

431

Artist: **Michael Klein**

Art Director: Dean Charlton

Client: Oracle Consulting

Medium: Ink, watercolor on watercolor paper

Size: 9" x 9"

432

Artist: **Leigh Wells**

Art Director: Angela Williams

Client: Levi Strauss & Co.

Medium: Mixed

Size: 25" x 18"

433

Artist: **Paul Cox**

Art Director: Richard Solomon

Client: Richard Solomon Artists Rep.

Medium: Watercolor on paper

Size: 20" x 16"

428

429

430

431

432

433

434

Artist: **Steve Turk**

Medium: Mixed on acetate

Size: 14" x 7"

435

Artist: **Jerry LoFaro**

Art Director: Cliff Stieglitz

Client: Airbrush Action Magazine

Medium: Acrylic on CS-10 board

Size: 18" x 12"

436

Artist: **Bill Mayer**

Art Director: David Whitmore

Client: Discovery Magazine

Medium: Dyes, gouache, airbrush on
       hot press board

Size: 12" x 10"

437

Artist: **Joe Sorren**

Art Director: John Davis

Client: Artragous

Medium: Acrylic on canvas

Size: 40" x 30"

438

Artist: **George Schill**

Medium: Acrylic on gessoed Kraft paper

Size: 10" x 8"

439

Artist: **Joe Sorren**

Art Director: Jeff Biggers

Client: Live Magazine

Medium: Acrylic on canvas

Size: 40" x 30"

434

435

436

437

438

439

462

Artist: **Gary Head**

Client: Hallmark Cards

Medium: Acrylic on board

Size: 20" x 13"

463

Artist: **Larry Moore**

Art Directors: Larry Moore, Steve Carsella

Client: Winter Park Autumn Art Festival

Medium: Pastel on paper

Size: 20" x 15"

462

463

UNCOMMISSIONED/UNPUBLISHED

JURY

CATEGORY CHAIRS
Steve Brodner
Al Lorenz
Jacqui Morgan
Barnett Plotkin

ANNUAL SHOW CHAIR
Vincent Di Fate

ASSISTANT CHAIR
Martha Vaughan

ILLUSTRATORS 40 CHAIR
Murray Tinkelman

464 GOLD MEDAL

Artist: **Dan Cosgrove**

Medium: Digital

Size: 18" x 13"

"This piece began as a drawing exercise. I wanted to figure out what the Golden Gate Bridge would look like from an aerial view. It wasn't until sometime later that I came up with the idea to use the bridge as a focal point for an updated version of the vintage travel poster. I am thrilled to receive this award from the Society of Illustrators."

465 GOLD MEDAL

Artist: **Loren Long**

Medium: Acrylic on board

Size: 16" x 14"

"Perhaps my first mistake was conjuring the romantic notion that I would give my two young sons paintings from Daddy for every birthday of their lives. In this case, I figured the two-year-old client, Griffith, would not mind my getting a portfolio sample out of the deal, so the result was this 1930s boxing scene. The referee is counting 'two' for my son's second birthday. For this effort to result in an award from the Society of Illustrators is truly thrilling. Griff, I guess you can keep the painting, but I'm keeping the medal."

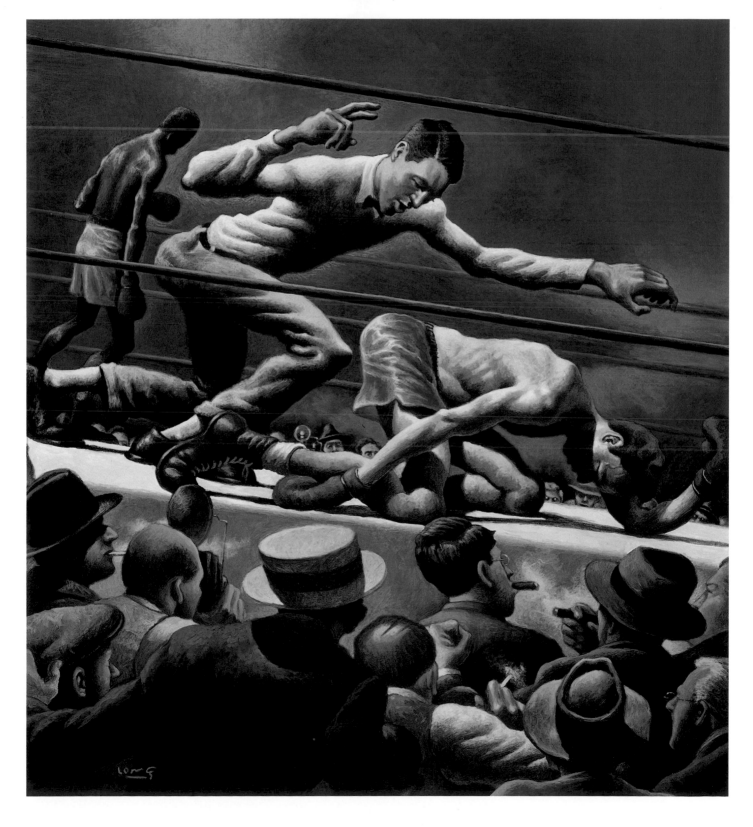

466 SILVER MEDAL

Artist: **Michael Garland**

Medium: Mixed, digital

"*ICARUS* is the story of a pig who longs to fly. It is my retelling of the original myth. It may also be a thinly veiled version of my own life. The art was done for a picture book idea that I was trying to sell. When the unpublished piece won this award, the project received the extra boost it needed. The book will be published next spring by Albert Whitman Publishers."

467

Artist: **Peter Fiore**

Medium: Oil on canvas

Size: 48" x 34"

468

Artist: **Francis Livingston**

Medium: Oil on board

Size: 12" x 9"

467

468

469

470

469

Artist: **Francis Livingston**

Medium: Oil on board

Size: 24" x 18"

470

Artist: **Francis Livingston**

Medium: Oil on board

Size: 24" x 18"

471

Artist: **Del-Bourree Bach**

Medium: Acrylic on canvas paper

Size: 16" x 22"

471

472

Artist: **Herbert Tauss**

Medium: Aqua-Oil on canvas

Size: 28" x 36"

473

Artist: **Brooks Burgan**

Medium: Oil on wood

Size: 20" x 22"

474

Artist: **Jean Hunter**

Medium: Oil on board

Size: 13" x 18"

475

Artist: **John C. Berkey**

Medium: Casein acrylic on board

Size: 22" x 16"

476

Artist: **Ray-Mel Cornelius**

Medium: Acrylic on canvas

Size: 30" x 40"

477

Artist: **David Gianfredi**

Medium: Oil on canvas

48" x 36"

478

Artist: **Murray Tinkelman**

Medium: Pen & ink on Bristol

Size: 20" x 16"

472

473

474

476

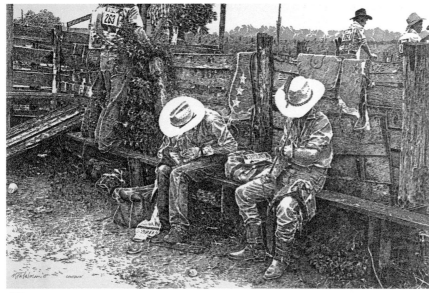

478

475

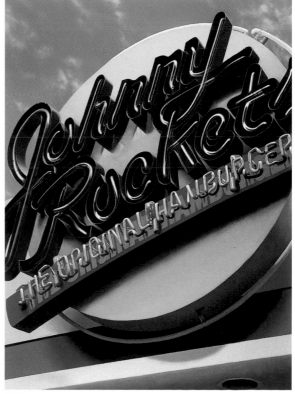

477

479

Artist: **Craig Tennant**

Medium: Oil on canvas

Size: 24" x 40"

480

Artist: **Craig Tennant**

Medium: Oil on canvas

Size: 30" x 50"

481

Artist: **Gary Aagaard**

Medium: Oil on canvas

Size: 36" x 24"

482

Artist: **Charly Palmer**

Medium: Acrylic, marbleized papers
on board

Size: 20" x 30"

483

Artist: **Ken Hamilton**

Medium: Watercolor on Lanaquarelle

Size: 15" x 11"

484

Artist: **Esti Silverberg**

Medium: Gouache on watercolor paper

Size: 17" x 11"

479

480

481

482

483

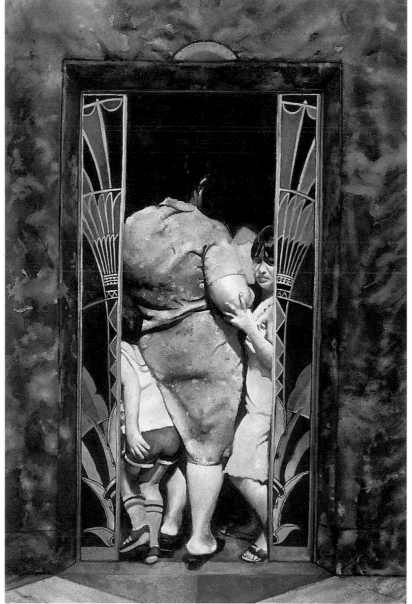

484

485

Artist: **George Thompson**

Medium: Mono print, ink, watercolor, pastel on paper

Size: 12" x 9"

486

Artist: **Pete Krein**

Medium: Pen & ink on paper

Size: 14" x 10"

487

Artist: **Tim O'Brien**

Medium: Oil on panel

Size: 12" x 8"

488

Artist: **Stephen L. Thompson**

Medium: Watercolor on Winsor Newton 140

Size: 20" x 15"

489

Artist: **Renée Reichert**

Medium: Pastel on watercolor paper

Size: 8" x 24"

490

Artist: **Tim O'Brien**

Medium: Oil on panel

Size: 21" x 15"

491

Artist: **Travis Dommermuth**

Medium: Mixed on board

Size: 16" x 14"

492

Artist: **Shayne Davidson**

Medium: Digital

Size: 9" x 6"

485

486

487

488

489

490

491

492

499

Artist: **Steve Reggiani**

Medium: Oil on masonite

Size: 14" x 34"

500

Artist: **Michael Whelan**

Medium: Acrylic on canvas

Size: 36" x 48"

501

Artist: **Martijn Heilig**

Medium: Mixed on board

Size: 4" x 5"

502

Artist: **Hiro Kimura**

Medium: Digital

Size: 15" x 10"

503

Artist: **David DeVries**

Medium: Mixed on board

Size: 16" x 7"

504

Artist: **Peter Fiore**

Medium: Oil on paper

Size: 20" x 14"

505

Artist: **Patrick Arrasmith**

Medium: Scratchboard

Size: 18" x 12"

499

500

501

502

503

504

505

506

Artist: **Michael Garland**

Medium: Mixed, digital

Size: 11" x 11"

507

Artist: **John Rush**

Medium: Oil on canvas

Size: 26" x26"

508

Artist: **Taylor McKimens**

Medium: Acrylic on paper

Size: 30" x 20"

509

Artist: **Lisa DiPietro**

Medium: Oil on canvas

Size: 20" x 16"

510

Artist: **Lucille Simonetti**

Medium: Colored pencil on Canson paper

Size: 15" x 12"

511

Artist: **Will Terry**

Medium: Acrylic on paper

Size: 16" x 12"

506

507

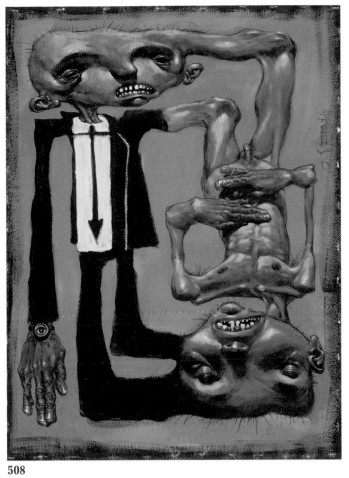

508

509

510

511

512

Artist: **Gene Greif**

Medium: Acrylic, pencil, crayon, collage on paper

Size: 10" x 10"

513

Artist: **Ekaterina Khromina**

Medium: Gouache on paper

Size: 10" x 17"

514

Artist: **Courtney Granner**

Medium: Mixed on watercolor paper

Size: 14" x 18"

512

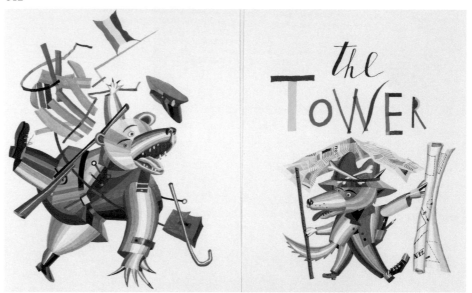

513

514

INTERNATIONAL

JURY

Jack Endewelt
Illustrator

Claire Moritz
Reader's Digest

Barbara Nessim
*Illustrator, Parsons School of
Design Illustration Chair*

Rodica Prado
Illustrator

James Yang
Illustrator

515

Artist: **James Bentley**

Medium: Mixed

Size: 11 cm x 8 cm

516

Artist: **Pol Turgeon**

Art Director: John Gudelj

Client: The Advertising & Design Club

Medium: Mixed

Size: 32 cm x 27 cm

517

Artist: **Ron Lightburn**

Client: Doubleday Canada Ltd.

Medium: Colored pencil

Size: 36 cm x 56 cm

518

Artist: **James Fryer**

Client: Artbank International

Medium: Acrylic on linen

Size: 42 cm x 57 cm

515

516

517

518

519

520

521

523

519
Artist: **Angela Whitaker**
Art Director: David Beaugeard
Client: Bath Spa University College
Medium: Watercolor

520
Artist: **Astrid Skaaren-Fystro**
Client: Teie Idretsforening
Size: 25 cm x 25 cm

521
Artist: **Giuliano Crivelli**
Client: Centre Swissair
Medium: Watercolor
Size: 60 cm x 60 cm

522
Artist: **John Morris**
Art Director: Allen Graham
Client: CPI Papers
Medium: Wood, mixed
Size: 90 cm x 40 cm x 25 cm

523
Artist: **Carl Ellis**
Art Directors: Rose Catt, Amy Jane Beer
Client: Wildlife of Britain Magazine
Medium: Pencil, watercolor
Size: 29 cm x 40 cm

522

524

Artist: **Louise Tarbutt**

Art Director: Emma Williams

Client: Woman and Home

Medium: Watercolor

Size: 25 cm x 28 cm

525

Artist: **Steve Adams**

Art Director: Kathleen Vandermoer

Client: McLean Hunter Publishing

Medium: Mixed

Size: 19 cm x 15 cm

526

Artist: **Simon Shaw**

Client: Watermar Ltd.

Medium: Oil

Size: 45 cm x 34 cm

527

Artist: **Stephen Braund**

Art Director; Jonathan Sheppard

Client: Atlantic Press

Medium: Ink

Size: 31 cm x 41 cm

528

Artist: **Hitoshi Miura**

Size: 103 cm x 73 cm

524

525

526

527

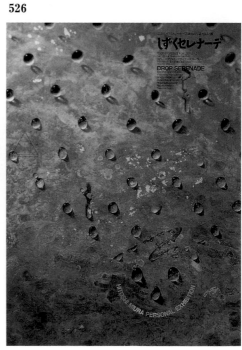

528

529

530

531

533

532

529

Artist: **Stephen Braund**

Art Director: Jonathan Sheppard

Client: Atlantic Press

Medium: Ink

Size: 28 cm x 60 cm

530

Artist: **Jamie Morris**

Medium: Oil on canvas

Size: 18 cm x 61 cm

531

Artist: **Mike McKeever**

Medium: Oil

532

Artist: **Carlos Puerta Cuevas**

Client: B Editorial

Medium: Watercolor on paper

Size: 34 cm x 25 cm

533

Artist: **Kunio Sato**

544

Artist: **Yasutaka Taga**

Art Director: Toshiaki Onogi

Client: Ja-mar Magazine

Medium: Digital

Size: 30 cm x 21 cm

545

Artist: **Rick Sealock**

Art Director: Joe Lepiand

Client: Identities Inc.

Medium: Mixed, acrylic

Size: 30 cm x 33 cm

546

Artist: **Carolyn Fisher**

Medium: Ink, digital

Size: 18 cm x 13 cm

547

Artist: **Cosa Dhers**

Art Director: Paul Bloemers

Client: Macfan

Medium: Oil on canvas

Size: 62 cm x 130 cm

548

Artist: **Douglas Fraser**

Art Director: Fraser Monaghan

Client: Canadian Pacific Railway

Medium: Alkyds on canvas

Size: 41 cm x 41 cm

549

Artist: **Jean-Manuel Duvivier**

Art Director: Christine Clessi

Client: Le Monde Diplomatique

Medium: Colored paper

Size: 15 cm x 18 cm

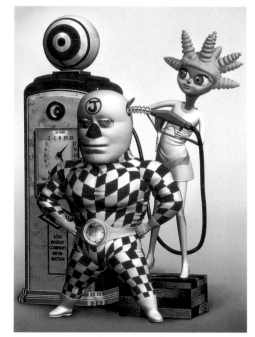

544

545

546

547

548

549

550

Artist: **Fabio Fernandes Cruz**

Art Director: Paulo Nascimento

Client: Gazeta Mercantil (newspaper)

Medium: Collage

Size: 7 cm x 25 cm

550

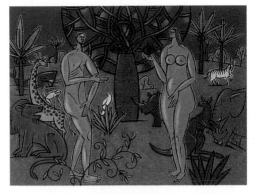

551

Artist: **Jean-Manuel Duvivier**

Art Director: Christine Clessi

Client: Le Monde Diplomatique

Medium: Colored paper

Size: 30 cm x 18 cm

552

Artist: **Hideki Mabuchi**

Art Director: Masakaazu Tanabe

Client: Gifu City

Medium: Acrylic, gouache on board

Size: 64 cm x 46 cm

553

Artist: **Jean-Manuel Duvivier**

Art Director: Christine Clessi

Client: Le Monde Diplomatique

Medium: Colored paper

Size: 19 cm x 20 cm

551

552

553

554

Artist: **Jaeeun Choi**

Art Director: Eui Do Huh

Client: Joongang Ilbo (Daily News)

Medium: Mixed

Size: 25 cm x 20 cm

554

555

Artist: **Kevin Hauff**

Art Director: Hazel Bennington

Client: PC Magazine

Medium: Acrylic on canvas

Size: 32 cm x 40 cm

556

Artist: **Scott Galley**

Art Director: Scott Thornley

Client: National Arts Centre

Medium: Pen & ink

Size: 12 cm x 10 cm

557

Artist: **Andrew Steward**

Art Director: Mark Wagstaff

Client: Mojo

Medium: Mixed

Size: 30 cm x 22 cm

558

Artist: **Paul Dallas**

Art Director: Jill Peters

Client: Zero Thru 9 Design Company

Medium: Watercolor

Size: 45 cm x 36 cm

559

Artist: **Brad Yeo**

Medium: Acrylic

Size: 33 cm x 28 cm

555

556

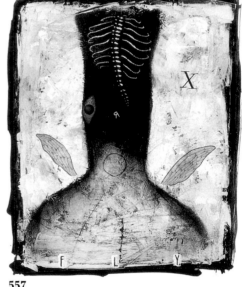

557

558

559

560

561

560

Artist: **Brad Yeo**

Medium: Acrylic

Size: 76 cm x 76 cm

561

Artist: **Jurgen Mick**

Medium: Colored pencil, ink

Size: 48 cm x 40 cm

562

Artist: **Horacio Guerriero**

Client: El Observador

Medium: Oil on canvas

Size: 60 cm x 80 cm

562

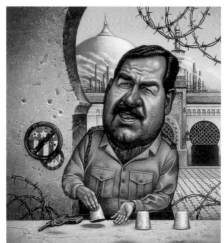

563

563

Artist: **Joseph Salina**

Art Director: Manfred Neussl

Client: Focus Magazine

Medium: Acrylic

Size: 26 cm x 26 cm

564

Artist: **Brad Yeo**

Medium: Acrylic

Size: 40 cm x 50 cm

565

Artist: **Joseph Salina**

Art Director: Manfred Neussl

Client: Focus Magazine

Medium: Acrylic

Size: 25cm x 26 cm

564

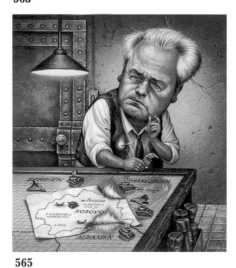

565

STUDENT SCHOLARSHIP COMPETITION

The Society of Illustrators fulfills its education mission through its museum exhibitions, library, archives, permanent collection and, most proudly, through the Student Scholarship Competition.

The following pages present a sampling of the 120 works selected from over 5,400 entries submitted by college level students nationwide.

The selections were made by a prestigious jury of professional illustrators.

Tim O'Brien chairs this program, and major financial support is given by Hallmark Corporate Foundation of Kansas City, Missouri. Along with donations from corporations, bequests and an annual auction of member-donated works, the Society awards over $80,000 to the students and their institutions.

This year, Murray Tinkelman was selected to receive the Distinguished Educator in the Arts award. This honor is now recognized by all as affirmation of an influential career in the classroom.

As you will see, the talent is there. If it is coupled with determination, these students will move ahead in this annual to join the selected professionals. Let's see.

SCHOLARSHIP COMMITTEE

Tim O'Brien, *Chairman*

Tim Bower
Lisa Cyr
Jerry Lofaro
Lauren Uram

SCHOLARSHIP JURY

Daniel Adel, *Illustrator*
Geri Bauer, *Jellybean Photographics*
Sean Beavers, *Illustrator*
Jim Bennett, *Illustrator*
Harry Bliss, *Illustrator*
Tom Bloom, *Illustrator*
Michelle Chang, *Illustrator*
Roy Comiskey, *Art Director*
Tim Coolbaugh, *Illustrator*
Nancy Doniger, *Illustrator*
Ingo Fast, *Illustrator*
Stanislaw Fernandes, *Illustrator*
Bob Field, *Illustrator*
Carter Goodrich, *Illustrator*
Josh Gosfield, *Illustrator*
David Lesh, *Illustrator*
Chris Motil, *Art Director (Scholastic, Inc.)*
Mike Mrak, *Art Director (Time Publications)*
Robert Sauber, *Illustrator*
Christopher Short, *Illustrator*
Carlos Torres, *Illustrator*
Martha Vaughan, *Illustrator*

HALLMARK CORPORATE FOUNDATION MATCHING GRANTS

The Hallmark Corporate Foundation of Kansas City, Missouri, is again this year supplying full matching grants for all of the awards in the Society's Student Scholarship Competition. Grants, restricted to the Illustration Departments, are awarded to the following institutions:

$12,000	School of Visual Arts
$8,000	Academy of Art College
$3,500	Art Center College of Design
$3,500	Paier College of Art
$3,500	University of the Arts
$2,500	Virginia Commonwealth University
$2,000	DuCret School of the Arts
$2,000	San Jose State University
$1,000	Montserrat College of Art
$1,000	Rhode Island School of Design
$1,000	Syracuse University

STUDENT SCHOLARSHIP COMPETITION

DISTINGUISHED EDUCATOR IN THE ARTS 1999

MURRAY TINKELMAN

Many of Murray Tinkelman's former students share similar memories of the teacher who would be instrumental in launching their careers. What they recall is his tremendous enthusiasm and boundless energy. "I first met Murray when he came to my school in Great Neck, Long Island," says award-winning illustrator Peter DeSève. "His slide presentation opened up the whole world of illustration. He was so passionate that his enthusiasm gave me the alibi I needed to pursue a career in the field." After graduation, DeSève enrolled at Parsons School of Design, where Tinkelman was head of the Illustration Department. "Murray was the fiercest proponent of illustration I've ever met," DeSève states. "He made it clear to me that I was in a noble profession."

Chris Spollen and Joe Ciardiello, now both successful illustrators, rode the ferry together from their homes on Staten Island to classes at the High School of Art and Design. "I would probably be in the fire department right now if it weren't for Murray coming to my high school, talking a mile a minute and telling me I could earn a living making pictures," laughs Spollen. "Murray's attitude was, 'If I can do it, you can do it,' and it was very infectious, very positive." After Tinkelman's lecture, both Spollen and Ciardiello decided to attend Parsons. "Murray was just inspiring to be around," Ciardiello remembers. "We learned not only from what he said but from the way he handled his own career, how he found projects that were of interest to him and how he promoted his ideas."

Murray Tinkelman is still busy promoting his ideas and maintaining a high-profile career. His many professional honors include Gold and Silver medals from the Society of Illustrators. Prestigious clients, including *The New York Times*, *The Ladies' Home Journal*, *American Heritage*, and

Boy's Life, have commissioned his work, and his illustrations have appeared on landmark series of book covers for Ballantine and Pocket Books. He has written and illustrated children's books, published articles on illustration, organized national shows, and been an active member of several professional organizations, all while maintaining his unmatched commitment to education.

Currently, Tinkelman is a Professor of Art and the Co-Director of the Independent Study Degree Program's Master of Arts in Illustration in the College of Visual and Performing Arts at Syracuse University. From a closet-sized office shared with colleague and former student Yvonne Buchanan, he runs an ambitious program and continues to guide and inspire students. "When I was

in high school, I brought my artwork to one of those Portfolio Days, and Murray Tinkelman was there," says Jennifer Szeto, a Junior at Syracuse, whose illustration "A Parody" is included in the 1999 Scholarship Exhibition. "His attitude was just so contagiously enthusiastic and such a boost. He was instrumental in my decision to attend Syracuse and to pursue my dream of becoming an artist."

Bunny Carter

This annual award is selected by the Board of Directors upon recommendation of the Education Committee.
Past recipients:
Alvin J. Pimsler 1997
Alan E. Cober 1998

Matthew Wygant
Steve Brennan, Instructor
Paier College of Art
Digital
$2,500 The Starr Foundation Award
RSVP Publication Award

Sterling C. Hundley
Robert Meganck, Instructor
Virginia Commonwealth University
Mixed
$2,500 The Starr Foundation Award

Zachary Baldus
Elizabeth Sayles, Instructor
School of Visual Arts
Acrylic
$1,000 Kirchoff/Wohlberg Award
in Memory of Frances Means

Ronald Bowman

Bunny Carter, Instructor

San Jose State University

Acrylic on board

$2,000 Howard and Jane Frank Foundation Science Fiction and Fantasy Award

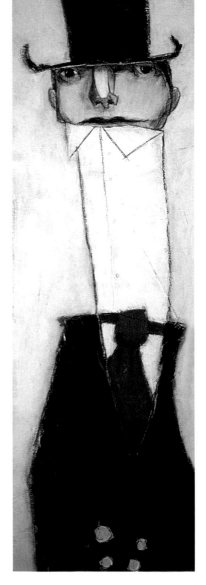

David Jon Kassan

Bob Dacey, Instructor

Syracuse University

Acrylic on board

$1,000 The Norman Rockwell Museum at Stockbridge Award

Joseph Hart

David Porter, Instructor

Rhode Island School of Design

Kris F. Grabowski
Ralph Giguere, Instructor
University of the Arts

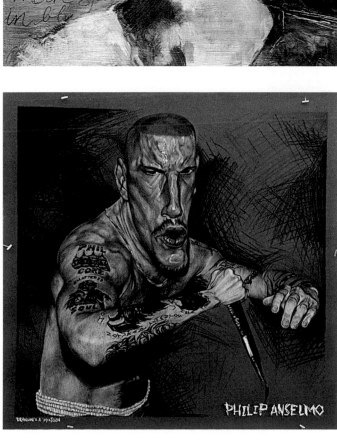

Brandon Miltgen
Jon McDonald, Instructor
Kendall College of Art & Design

Phung Huynh
Aaron Smith, Instructor
Art Center College of Design

Jason DeLancey
Bob Hochgertel, Instructor
Pennsylvania School of Art & Design

Pete Dunbar
Doug Anderson, Instructor
University of Hartford

Jason Specht
Traci Haymans, Instructor
Savannah College of Art & Design

ARTISTS INDEX

INTERNATIONAL ARTISTS INDEX

PROFESSIONAL STATEMENTS & SOCIETY ACTIVITIES

Put "art" back in art director.
Use illustration as a solution.

© JOE SORREN

LIFE, DEATH, LOSS, MYSTERY, WONDER, SILLINESS, IN TWO DIMENSIONS. TRYING TO LIVE UP TO THAT EVERY DAY WITH BRUSHES AND PAINT HELPS FEAR... MAKE THIS AN AMAZING JOB.

PAUL MICICH 515-981-4707 796 COOLIDGE ST, NORWALK IA 50211

Fred Harper © '99/The American Spectator June Cover, www.f-red.net **(718) 855-1305**

Where to find the best illustrators in the business.

Perfect for producers of books, clothing, music, greeting cards, games, electronic media, animation houses, and advertising agencies, *Picturebook* is the only sourcebook targeted to artwork created especially for children. Finally, a way for children's book illustrators to effectively show their work, and a source for publishers to find the perfect artist is simple.

"My delight in *Picturebook* is that it gets the images we want in front of exactly the people we want to see them. Year after year *Picturebook* has worked for us. Thanks to *Picturebook*, I have very happy artists working on very wonderful projects. I have even received surprise calls from places that I didn't expect to get calls from offering very interesting projects!

—Pat Lindgren, Lindgren & Smith

For information on being included in the next issue, please contact us or go to our website. For publishers or art buyers not receiving this annual volume, please call to qualify for your free issue.

www.picture-book.com   email: info@picture-book.com
2080 Valleydale Road, Suite 15, Birmingham, AL 35244
(888) 490-0100 (205)403-9882 Fax: (205) 403-9162

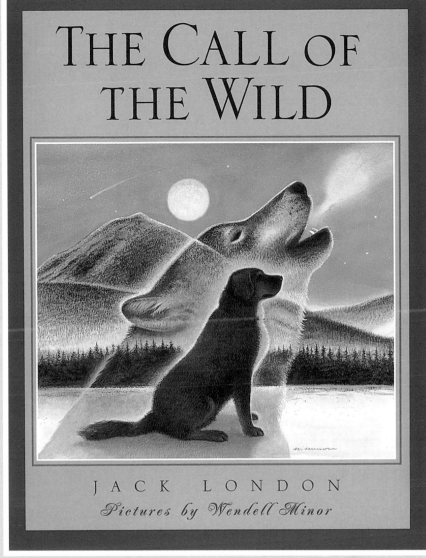

Illustration by N. Ascencios, Represented by Gerald & Cullen Rapp, Inc.
Showcase Illustration 22, page 16-17

To all of you that wield a pencil and
a glass of merlot with equal finesse – we salute you.

ZOË VILES
2 1 2 . 7 7 4 . 7 4 6 6

Great Illustrators Represent Gerald & Cullen Rapp

Beth Adams

Philip Anderson

N. Ascencios

Garin Baker

Stuart Briers

Lon Busch

Jonathan Carlson

R. Gregory Christie

Jack Davis

Robert de Michiell

The Dynamic Duo

Randall Enos

Leo Espinosa

Phil Foster

Mark Fredrickson

Mark Gagnon

Eliza Gran

Thomas Hart

Peter Horvath

David Hughes

Celia Johnson

Douglas Jones

James Kaczman

Steve Keller

J.D. King

Laszlo Kubinyi

Scott Laumann

Davy Liu

PJ Loughran

Bernard Maisner

Hal Mayforth

Marlies Najaka

James O'Brien

John Pirman

Jean-Francois Podevin

Marc Rosenthal

Alison Seiffer

Seth

Jeffrey Smith

James Steinberg

Drew S.

Elizabeth Traynor

Michael Witte

Noah Woods

Brad Yeo

And Gerald & Cullen Rapp Has Represented Great Illustrators Since 1944.

108 East 35th Street   New York, NY 10016   **Gerald & Cullen Rapp, Inc.**   Phone: 212-889-3337   Fax: 212-889-3341

ILLUSTRATION   BOOKS FOR CHILDREN
BOX 699 JAMESPORT   NEW YORK 11947
(631) 722 4322   NFORKART@AOL.COM

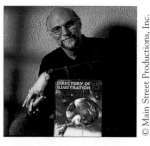

Building { 2 Million · 2,000,000 · Bonds } A Year

ALL IMAGES COPYRIGHT TOM WHITE.IMAGES

TOM WHITE.IMAGES *phone* 212.866.7841 *website* www.twimages.com

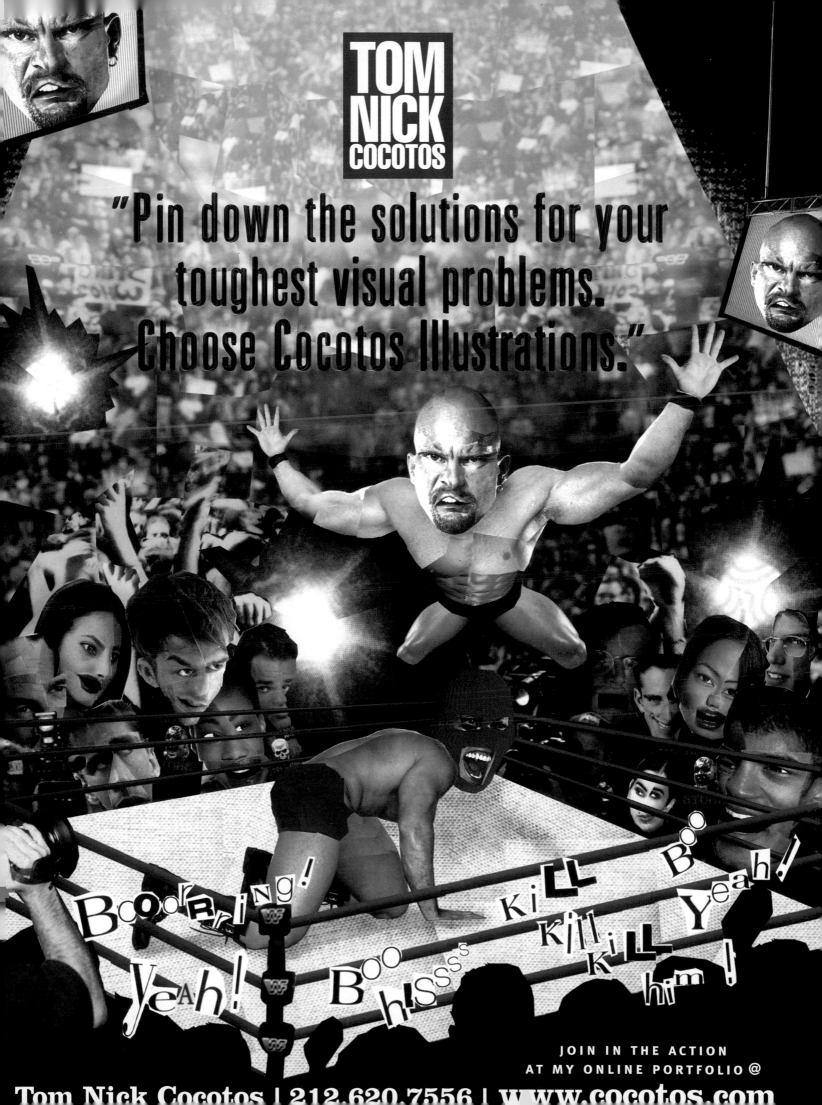

OUR OWN SHOW *1999*

10th Anniversary

STEVAN
DOHANOS
AWARD
Robert E. McGinnis

THE SOCIETY OF ILLUSTRATORS
MEMBERS TENTH ANNUAL
OPEN EXHIBITION

AWARD OF MERIT
John Thompson

AWARD OF MERIT
Thomas Wise

"Our Own Show" presents annually the Stevan Dohanos Award
as the Best in Show in this open, unjuried exhibition.

JURY

Robert Berran, Ted Lewin, Joseph Montebello, Jacques Parker

Our Own Show

10th Anniversary

THE ORIGINAL ART 1999

SILVER
Illustrator: *Petra Mathers*
Book: Lottie's New Friend
Art Director: Ann Bobco
Editor: Anne Schwartz
Publisher: Simon & Schuster
Children's Publishing Division

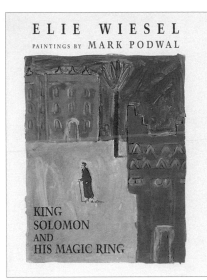

SILVER
Illustrator: *Mark Podwal*
Book: King Solomon and
His Magic Ring
Art Director: Ava Weiss
Editor: Susan Hirschman
Publisher: Greenwillow Books

GOLD
Illustrator: *Jon J Muth*
Book: Come On, Rain!
Art Director: David J. Saylor
Editor: Dianne Hess
Publisher: Scholastic Press

Founded in 1980 to "Celebrate the Fine Art of Children's Book Illustration,"
this exhibition has been sponsored by the Society of Illustrators
for the past nine years.

The selection process was by a jury of outstanding illustrators, art directors
and editors in the field of children's book publishing.

JURY
Raul Colon ◆ Claire Counihan ◆ Yumi Heo
G. Brian Karas ◆ Barbara McClintock ◆ Elise Primavera ◆ Chris Sheban

Brian Pinkney CHAIR, "The Original Art 1999" ◆ Dilys Evans FOUNDER, "The Original Art"

The Society of Illustrators recognizes the underwriting support of The Picture Book

THE DAVID P. USHER/GREENWICH WORKSHOP MEMORIAL AWARD

⟁

JOHN RUSH

"THE STEELWORKER"

This is the first of an annual award to be named in memory of the founder of The Greenwich Workshop.

The selection was made from all of the works exhibited in the 41st Annual. The jury included: Past Gold Medalists Jerry Pinkney and Michael Deas; Exhibition Chair, Vincent Di Fate; and representing The Greenwich Workshop, Scott Usher and Pete Landa. A cash prize and subsequent print edition accompanies the award.

THE GREENWICH WORKSHOP

Since 1972

SOCIETY OF ILLUSTRATORS MUSEUM SHOP

The Society of Illustrators Museum of American Illustration maintains a shop featuring many quality products. Four-color, large format books document contemporary illustration and the great artists of the past. Museum quality prints and posters capture classic images. T-shirts, sweatshirts, hats, mugs and tote bags make practical and fun gifts.

The Museum Shop is an extension of the Society's role as the center for illustration in America today. For further information or quantity discounts, contact the Society at
TEL: (212) 838-2560 / FAX: (212) 838-2561
EMail: society@societyillustrators.org

ILLUSTRATORS 41   **NEW!**
270 pp.
Cover by John Rush.
Contains 510 works of art.
Included are Hall of Fame biographies
and the Hamilton King interview.
Our most recent annual, the most contemporary illustration.
$49.95

ILLUSTRATORS ANNUAL BOOKS

These catalogs are based on our annual juried exhibitions, divided into four major categories in American Illustration: Editorial, Book, Advertising, and Institutional. Some are available in a limited supply only.

In addition, a limited number of out-of-print collector's editions of the Illustrators Annuals that are not listed below (1959 to Illustrators 30) are available as is.

Contact the Society for details...

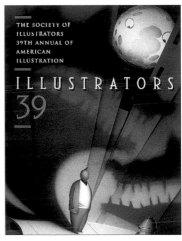

ILLUSTRATORS 40
$40.00

ILLUSTRATORS 39
$40.00

ILLUSTRATORS 38
$40.00

ILLUSTRATORS 37
$30.00

ILLUSTRATORS 36
$25.00

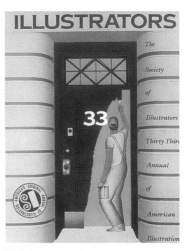

ILLUSTRATORS 33
$20.00

SOCIETY OF ILLUSTRATORS • 128 East 63rd Street • New York, NY 10021-7303
www.societyillustrators.org   EMail: society@societyillustrators.org

Raul Colòn

Jerry Pinkney

Guy Billout

Fred Otnes

ARTISTS FEATURED IN THE SERIES:

EDITORIAL

Marshall Arisman
Guy Billout
Alan E. Cober
Elaine Duillo
Joan Hall
Wilson McLean
Barbara Nessim
Tim O'Brien
Mel Odom

ADVERTISING

N. Ascencios
Mark Borow
Robert M. Cunningham
Teresa Fasolino
Mark Hess
Hiro Kimura
Rafal Olbinski
Fred Otnes
Chris Spollen

CHILDREN'S BOOKS

Steve Byram
Raul Colòn
Laura Cornell
Steve Kroninger
Emily McCully
James McMullan
Jerry Pinkney
Charles Santore
Dan Yaccarino

PRO-ILLUSTRATION

by Jill Bossert

A How-to Series

$24.00 EACH. SET OF THREE $60.00

VOLUME ONE
EDITORIAL ILLUSTRATION

The Society of Illustrators has simulated an editorial assignment for a Sunday magazine supplement surveying the topic of "Love." Topics assigned to the illustrators include: Erotic Love, First Love, Weddings, Sensual Love, Computer Love, Adultery and Divorce. The stages of execution. from initial sketch to finish, are shown in a series of photographs and accompanying text. It's a unique, behind-the-scenes look at each illustrator's studio and the secrets of their individual styles. Professional techniques demonstrated include oil, acrylic, collage, computer, etching, trompe l'oeil, dyes and airbrush.

Joan Hall

Chris Spollen

VOLUME TWO
ADVERTISING ILLUSTRATION

This is an advertising campaign for a fictitious manufacturer of timepieces. The overall concept is "Time" and nine of the very best illustrators put their talents to solving the problem. The stages of execution, from initial phone call to finish, are described in photographs and text. You'll understand the demonstration of the techniques used to create a final piece of art. Professional techniques demonstrated include oil, acrylic, mixed media collage, computer, three-dimension and airbrush.

VOLUME THREE
CHILDREN'S BOOKS

In photographs and text, each of the nine artists describe the stages of execution from initial idea--if they are the author, too--or manuscript proposed by an editor, to the completion of a piece of art. They discuss the special challenges of creating children's books, among them: consistency of character and tone, attention to pace and visual flow, and the task of serving narrative as well as aesthetics.

Charles Santore

Maxfield Parrish • J. C. Leyendecker • Norman Rockwell • N. C. Wyeth • James Montgomery Flagg • Dean Cornwell
Harold Von Schmidt • Al Parker • Robert Fawcett • Stevan Dohanos • Tom Lovell • Charles Dana Gibson
Bernie Fuchs • Winslow Homer • Robert Peak • Coby Whitmore • Frederic Remington • Howard Chandler Christy
John Clymer • Mark English • Charles Marion Russell • Rockwell Kent • Al Hirschfeld • Haddon Sundblom
Maurice Sendak • René Bouché • Robert T. McCall • John Held, Jr. • Burt Silverman • Jessie Willcox Smith • Joe Bowler
Dorothy Hood • Robert McGinnis • Thomas Nast • Coles Phillips • Ben Shahn • McClelland Barclay
and many, many more

"The Glen," illustration for Brown & Bigelow calendar, 1938. Photo courtesy of the Archives of the American Illustrators Gallery, New York City.

"Jack and the Giant," cover illustration for Collier's magazine. Collection of American Illustrators Gallery, New York City.

"The Botanist," cover illustration for Collier's, July 18, 1908. Collection of American Illustrators Gallery, New York City.

"Villa Gori, Siena," illustration for Italian Villas and Their Gardens, 1904. Collection of the Society of Illustrators Museum of American Illustration.

"The Glen," illustration for Brown & Bigelow calendar, 1938. Photo courtesy of the Archives of the American Illustrators Gallery, New York City.

Design for the Century Mid-Summer Holiday Number, August, 1897. Photo courtesy of the Archives of the American Illustrators Gallery, New York City.

"Garden of Allah," decoration for gift boxes of Crane's Chocolates, 1918. Photo courtesy of the Archives of the American Illustrators Gallery, New York City

62

63

FAMOUS AMERICAN ILLUSTRATORS

NEW!
by Arpi Ermoyan

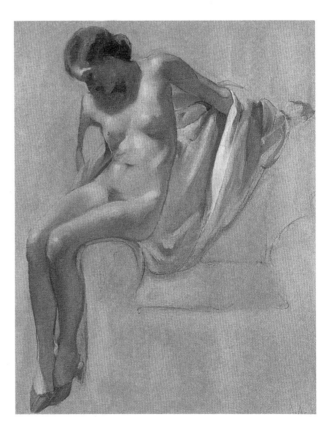

THE HALL OF FAME

Every year since the inception of the Hall of Fame in 1958, the Society of Illustrators bestows its highest honor upon those artists recognized for their distinguished achievement in the art of illustration. The 87 recipients of the Hall of Fame Award represented in this book are the foremost illustrators of the last two centuries.

FAMOUS AMERICAN ILLUSTRATORS, a full-color, 224 page volume, is a veritable "Who's Who" of American illustration. The artists are presented in the order in which they were elected to the Hall of Fame. Included are short biographical sketches and major examples of each artist's work. Their range of styles is all-encompassing, their viewpoints varied, their palettes imaginative. The changing patterns of life in America are vividly recorded as seen through the eyes of these men and women—the greatest illustrators of the 19th and 20th Centuries. **11 1-2 x 12 inches. $39.95**

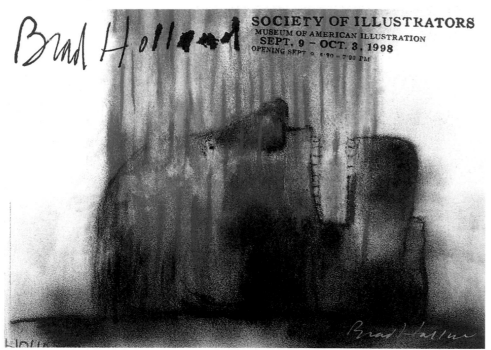

BRAD HOLLAND EXHIBITION 1998 - 34" x 24" $20.00

42nd ANNUAL - Kinuko Craft -
17" x 22" $10.00

THE DIGITAL SHOW - Steve Lyons
15" x 27" $10.00

EDWIN AUSTIN ABBEY 25" x 22" $10.00

KENNETH PAUL BLOCK - 14 x 23 $10.00
Retrospective Exhibition

POSTERS

The Society has created some of the most exciting and enjoyable posters around to announce their exhibitions. Subjects are both contemporary and historic. All are full color and are printed on premium stock.

The set of 7 posters: $40.00

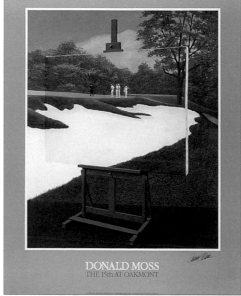

DONALD MOSS
22" x 28"
$10.00

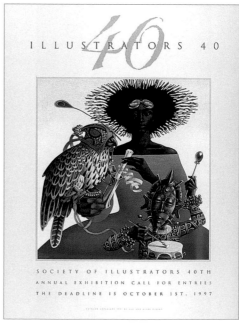

40TH ANNUAL
Leo & Diane Dillon
18" x 24" $10.00

THE BUSINESS OF ILLUSTRATION
Steve Heller's effective text on the nuts and bolts and whys of illustration. Commentary by leading pros and agents as well as hints on pricing and self-promotion. Great for students and young professionals. Recommended highly.
144 pages, softbound, color **$27.50**

GOING DIGITAL
AN ARTIST'S GUIDE TO COMPUTER ILLUSTRATION
At last, an easy-to-read guide to illustrating on your computer. Author and illustrator, John Ennis, offers an under- the-hood look at how it's done and how to start up your digital studio.
144 pages, softbound, color. **$29.95**

HEALTH HAZARDS MANUAL
A comprehensive review of materials and supplies, from fixatives to pigments, airbrushes to solvents.
132 pages, softbound. **$9.95**

THE BUSINESS LIBRARY

Each of these volumes is a valuable asset to the professional artist whether established or just starting out. Together they form a solid base for your business.

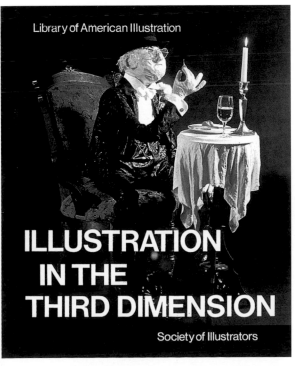

ILLUSTRATION IN THE THIRD DIMENSION
27 artists explain just how dimensional art works. Media include woods, metals, fabrics, resins and junk. This 1978 classic is still an effective look at this genre.
112 pages,hardbound, limited color. **$12.00**

THE LEGAL GUIDE FOR THE VISUAL ARTIST
1999 EDITION.
Tad Crawford's text explains basic copyrights, moral rights, the sale of rights, taxation, business accounting and the legal support groups available to artists.
256 pages, softbound. **$19.95**

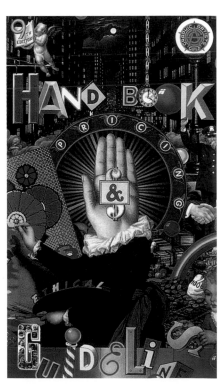

GRAPHIC ARTISTS GUILD HANDBOOK PRICING AND ETHICAL GUIDELINES - VOL. 9
Includes an outline of ethical standards and business practices, as well as price ranges for hundreds of uses and sample contracts.
312 page, softbound. **$24.95**

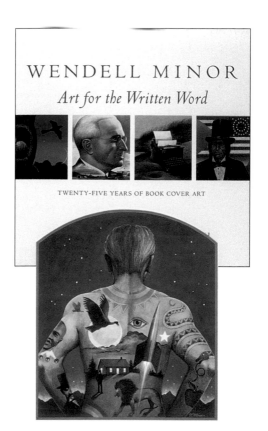

WENDELL MINOR
ART FOR THE WRITTEN WORD

A retrospective of this award-winning artist's book cover art. Includes an introduction by David McCullough and commentary by the authors.
154 pages, color, softbound.
$30.00

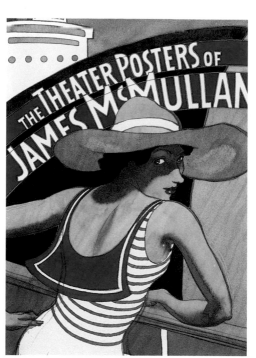

THE THEATER POSTERS OF
JAMES MCMULLAN

A celebration of his memorable posters, most commissioned by New York's Lincoln Center Theater. Includes reproductions of preliminary sketches and photo reference, as well as the finished art.
128 pages, color, hardbound. **$35.95**

SIGHT & INSIGHT -
THE ART OF BURTON SILVERMAN

From the exhibition held at the Butler Institute of American Art in Youngstown, Ohio and the Brigham Young Museum in Provo, UT, 1999. This book is a collection of the past 25 years of work by this universally respected painter, illustrator and teacher.
157 pages, color, hardbound. **$35.95**

BOOKS & CATALOGS

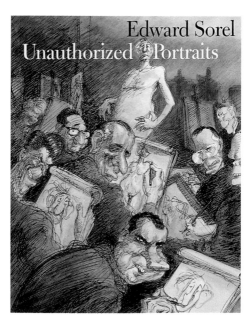

EDWARD SOREL -
UNAUTHORIZED PORTRAITS

Featuring satirical caricatures of the famous and infamous. Each of the book's three sections - "History", "Entertainment and the Arts", and "Politics" has a wry autobiographical section, and every drawing has its own informative caption.
173 pages, color, hardbound. **$40.00**

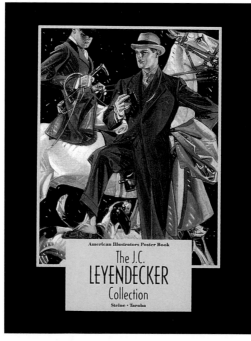

THE J. C. LEYENDECKER COLLECTION

Collector's Press poster edition offering 18 plates all from the original art with accompanying text by Fred Taraba. An outstanding addition for the discerning collector.
22 pages, color. 10" x 14". **$24.95**

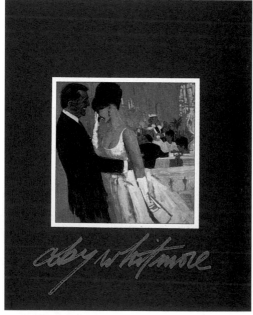

COBY WHITMORE

The good life of the 1950s and 1960s as illustrated in the Ladies Home Journal, McCall's and Redbook.
12 pages, color, softbound. **$16.00**

APPAREL

SI CAPS
Blue or Red with SI logo and name embroidered in white.
Adjustable, one size fits all
$15.

White shirt with the Society logo.
L, XL, XXL **$15.**

39TH ANNUAL EXHIBITION "CALL" T-SHIRT
Image of the tattooed face by Anita Kunz.
100% cotton. Heavyweight pocket T.
L, XL, XXL **$15.**

38TH ANNUAL EXHIBITION "CALL" T-SHIRT
Image of a frog on a palette by Jack Unruh.
Frog on front pocket.
100% cotton. Heavyweight pocket T.
L, XL, XXL **$15.**

NAVY BLUE MICROFIBER NYLON CAP
SI logo and name embroidered in white. Floppy
style cap. Feels broken in before its even worn.
Adjustable, one size fits all.
$20.

SWEATSHIRTS
Blue with white lettering of multiple
logos or grey with large red SI.
L, XL, XXL **$20.**

40TH ANNUAL EXHIBITION "CALL" T-SHIRT
Image of "The Messenger" by Leo and Diane Dillon.
100% cotton. Heavyweight pocket T.
L, XL, XXL **$15.**

GIFT ITEMS

SI LAPEL PINS
Actual Size
$6.00

The Society's famous Red and Black logo, designed by Bradbury Thompson, is featured on many items.

SI TOTE BAGS
Heavyweight, white canvas bags are 14" high with the two-color logo **$15.00**

SI PATCH
White with blue lettering and piping - 4" wide
$4.00

SI CERAMIC COFFEE MUGS
Heavyweight 14 oz. mugs feature the Society's logo or original illustrations from the Permanent Collection.
1. John Held, Jr.'s "Flapper";
2. Norman Rockwell's "Dover Coach";
3. J. C. Leyendecker's "Easter";
4. Charles Dana Gibson's "Gibson Girl"
5. SI Logo
$6.00 each

SI NOTE CARDS
Norman Rockwell greeting cards, 3-7/8" x 8-5/8", inside blank, great for all occasions. Includes 100% rag envelopes

10 CARDS	**- $10.00**
20 CARDS	**- $18.00**
50 CARDS	**- $35.00**
100 CARDS	**- $60.00**

ORDER FORM

Mail: The Museum Shop, Society of Illustrators, 128 East 63rd Street, New York, NY 10021-7303
Phone: 1-800-SI-MUSEUM (1-800-746-8738) Fax: 1-212-838-2561 EMail: society@societyillustrators.org

41

NAME _____

COMPANY _____

STREET _____
(No P.O. Box numbers please)

CITY _____

STATE _____ ZIP _____

PHONE ( ) _____

Enclosed is my check for $ _____
Make checks payable to SOCIETY OF ILLUSTRATORS

Please charge my credit card:
☐ **American Express** ☐ **Master Card** ☐ **Visa**

CARD NUMBER _____

SIGNATURE _____ EXPIRATION DATE _____
*please note if name appearing on the card is different than the mailing name.

Ship via FEDEX Economy and charge my account _____

QTY	DESCRIPTION	SIZE	COLOR	PRICE	TOTAL

# of items ordered	Total price of item(s) ordered	
	TAX (NYS Residents add 8 1/4%)	
	UPS Shipping per order	**6.00**
	or	
	Foreign Shipping via Surface per order	**15.00**
	or	
	Foreign Shipping via Air per order	CONTACT OFFICE
		FX
	TOTAL DUE	